Stories From the Career Couch

Stories From the Career Couch

Inspiring personal narratives and expert insight that will enable you to enjoy a fulfilling career

SUSIE LAWRENCE

THE CHOIR PRESS

First published in the United Kingdom in 2023 by
The Choir Press

ISBN 978-1-78963-375-4

Contents

Introduction

> The future belongs to those who believe in the beauty of their dreams.
>
> Eleanor Roosevelt

What do you want to do when you "grow up"? We all remember that question from countless relatives and well-meaning adults. What do you want to 'be' when you grow up is actually a much more interesting word than 'do' as it implies an examination of how you think, feel and behave as you live and work. Perhaps the question is now redundant in a world where the average graduate will have five different careers and the backdrop to our working lives is so fluid. Our working world of today requires a constant telling and retelling of our life story, creating possibilities and new narratives.

I am a psychologist specialising in work and career and love what I do. The majority of my work is with individual clients, supporting them as they explore what career means to them. This is often combined with a focus on flourishing in a particular role, commissioned by the organisation they work for. It is now the thirteenth year of running my practice and I have worked with over 300 individuals. Clients will spend on average ten hours with me, across a period of months, practising, reflecting and experimenting with new ways of behaving, interspersed with our monthly meetings. My clients may have reached a point in their working life where they are restless and want to explore why work might have lost its meaning. They want to look back and then create a tangible set of possibilities for the future. Other clients are supported by their organisations to hone their leadership and explore how they contribute to the team and how they build relationships.

I finish so many sessions with my clients moved by the joy and pain of being human. Moved by their courage, perseverance, imagination, frustration, shame, compassion and search for purpose. And mostly moved by the desire for reflection and the hope for the future. Career conversations are rich and demand much from my clients. As if life was ever as easy as picking a job that might suit us and doing this until we retire! Our work together looks forward positively and is solutions-focused. It is also work that necessitates trusting clients to challenge obstacles that they might put in their way. It supports them to develop new ways of thinking and feeling. The territory of 'self' can feel close to the work of a therapist but this sits at the heart of any career work. We all carry narratives, misperceptions and limitations that sit alongside our strengths and future plans. It's fascinating to explore the mystery that goes on in our heads and its relationship with the outside world.

This book tells twelve stories written by twelve of my career-coaching clients. Clients who have been committed to having brave conversations and have the desire to improve and change aspects of their career. These are real people and so life is messy and complicated and doesn't always meet expectations. These are 'regular' people experiencing 'regular' lives and they illuminate experiences and themes that will resonate with each reader. The clients aren't writers, so what you will read is raw and each story has a style and feel of its own. Each piece gives us an insight into how each person conceives the reality of work and what they initiate to shape this reality. These stories are about developing self-belief and exploring our psychology; how we feel think and behave about and at work. They are about developing the capacity to empathise and to influence change. They are about developing meaningful and trusting relationships in the office. They are about success but also about vulnerability and how it feels when life doesn't quite go according to plan.

Each client essay in the book is followed by a chapter written by me reflecting on the themes the client has explored and connecting this story to other client experiences. I hope these themes will challenge you to reflect on your own career. As a business psychologist, I am privileged to have worked with clients who bring a diversity of experience and perspectives into my consulting room. I see the world through the eyes of my clients and we both commit to being open-minded and embracing new perspectives. This book will connect the deeply personal to the more universal and I hope will resonate with your own experiences.

How do you develop the emotional agility to create successful behaviours? How can you set intentions and be productive? What does it mean to break away from perfectionism? Does work have to feel passionate? What does a balanced life look like? How do you retain your energy and cope when things become more challenging? What does courage look like? These are just some of the many questions I will explore in my responses to the clients' stories.

I hope the book will inspire, provoke and support you to reflect on what career means to you and how you might challenge yourself to do things differently.

CHAPTER ONE

Getting Unstuck

ANGELA

In pure cliché, I was a year away from thirty when I realised my situation was untenable. At the time I was in a good, well-paying position with a great pension and decent hours. My colleagues were friendly and supportive, and the work I did was important, good work that helped advance scientific research. It was, in short, a brilliant job – for someone else. I tried to imagine doing the same kind of work for another thirty years, and felt sick at the idea. But there was a problem. The idea of leaving felt almost as bad. The job was safe, and stable. There was a salary ladder I could climb, a professional path I could follow. And what would I even do – a decade of experience behind me in a field I did not care for. I felt entirely stuck.

I have always loved stories. As a child, I would construct complicated storylines in my head that I would play out on my own in the back garden. I would be a warrior princess, or a spy, or an elf living in the trees. I was quite happy to play for long hours in the sole company of my imagination.

My love affair with my own imagination has never really stopped, though it's certainly stalled at times. Throughout my childhood I regularly wrote stories for fun, making little books of folded paper which I filled with crayoned illustrations. When I got older, I read more and widely, and excelled in English literature. I joined a drama club, and loved spending Saturday mornings inhabiting other bodies, speaking other people's words and recreating their stories.

Storytelling, then, came naturally to me, and reading and analysing the stories of others was pleasurable and easy. And when, as I progressed through school, it became more challenging, I enjoyed the challenge. But I made the fatal mistake of believing that because I found these things easier than other subjects at school, everyone must find them easier, and that, in fact, they weren't hard at all.

Through a mix of family, school and media influence, I had come to believe that the only work that had merit was work that was hard. If I could complete an essay or exam with relative ease, and if I actually enjoyed the process, it felt to me less of an achievement than if I had had to really struggle with both content and motivation. The subjects I did find difficult – Chemistry, Maths, Physics – were things I was not naturally adept at. I was, however, able to do well at them because I was clever, and because I applied myself in pursuit of grades and praise. And by my incorrect logic – where work was, by definition, supposed to be hard and dull – I presumed that excelling at these was the real sign of my academic worth. What's more, these were frequently touted by school and the "Mickey Mouse degree obsessed" media as sensible, worthy subjects. These were subjects that looked good on a UCAS form and a CV, that opened a door to any job you could ever dream of. Drama and story writing were fine hobbies, but they weren't careers.

At the same time as growing up with stories, I had also grown up around nature. I loved animals and flowers and trees, so when a Biomedical Sciences degree was suggested as a good fit for my A levels, I thought why not? I might one day get a job working with animals, and even if I didn't, I'd have that 'good' degree on my CV. I got a place at a Russell Group university, and though I felt sad at the prospect of leaving behind the study of stories, I knew that I could always read books and see plays for fun. Off I went, with my new textbooks weighing down my suitcases, ready for that academic and career success I had been told would surely follow my wise choices.

It did not take me long to realise that I was not suited to Biomedical Sciences. I have since learned that when you have a passion for a subject, it is much easier to push yourself to do well, to learn, to succeed even when it's difficult. When you care little for a subject, finding the motivation to study when topics get tough is much, much harder. And sciences at university were tough. Harder than they had been at school, and with little organic interest I floundered. I barely scraped passes in most subjects, and with each set of exam results my self-esteem plummeted. I could never seem to hold in my head all the facts and figures required for exam questions, I could not make the connections between ideas that were necessary in essays, I could not follow the lab demonstrations. I considered dropping out multiple times, but that felt too much like failing. Again, with hindsight, that would have been a much braver choice than battling through with my average grades.

This was the beginning of a decade of working in the sciences, mostly in communications. This was an attempt to move back towards that thing I had always loved – storytelling. Perhaps, I reasoned, I could tell stories about science. This worked to an extent. Being out in the real working world was a marked improvement on university life. My jobs required a wider view of science than my very focused degree had allowed. I did get to write a little – blog posts, articles – and while I didn't love the subject matter, I could at least express some of that creative writing talent. And in my spare time I began to jot down short stories, plays, and poems but rarely finished them, and certainly never showed them to anyone.

As the years ticked away I moved from job to job. In my first role I was quickly promoted, and my salary grew. I saw this as a sign of success, even as I felt disinterested in and dismissive of my work. This interpretation of success stuck, and without a particular passion for my work, I made career choices based not on interest, but on money and status. I would take a job for the salary and the title, but quickly grow bored in the new role, and frustrated at the limitations of my work. I would move on to new posts in new organisations, hoping that each would be the job that finally felt right, only to stay just long enough to build up enough experience to apply elsewhere. Getting hired, and being handed bulkier paycheques, became a proxy for the life satisfaction I sought, a way of reassuring myself that I was getting somewhere, moving forward. I may have disliked the work I was doing day to day, but at least I earned decent money. At least I could go out for nice dinners, buy nice clothes, call myself a manager, be in charge of a team. I was climbing a career ladder that I did not want to be on, and my only reward was more responsibility for work that I struggled to invest in.

All this time, I think I knew what I really wanted to do. I suppose I had always known, but by this point – a decade since I stopped studying books and creating stories – I was too scared to try. I still had stored, in notebooks and on my computer, hundreds of half-finished novels, poems, plays. But I had convinced myself that it was too late to go down the route of a creative career, especially with no formal training or literary background. I was nearly out of my twenties, married with a mortgage – it felt like the worst time to take a risk.

I had been told, once, that the route to a creative career was to get a good job and financial security, and develop your creative work in your spare time. But as I had got older, my work and financial and social commitments had only increased, so that this elusive spare time had, year by year, become sparer than ever. The financial commitments, too, only became greater – first increasing rents in the city and travel costs for work, and then mortgage payments – so that the need for security had always increased, not diminished.

Perhaps more fundamentally, the biggest harm to my creative output was my weariness. Contrary to the myth of the struggling artist, unhappiness is not conducive to creativity. Working a job that I found unstimulating and frustrating left me drained at the end of each day so that I would come home after work with just enough energy to pour a glass of wine and watch hours of Netflix.

That was when my sister-in-law suggested I try coaching. She mentioned a friend who had been in a similar situation, who had found her way forward with professional help. I'd never tried coaching before, and had, if anything, thought it a little self-indulgent. Here I was, with a perfectly good job and the good fortune of a high-level education, someone with choices many are denied, asking for more.

But I also knew that I needed someone impartial to step in and help me work out what I was doing wrong, why I kept taking jobs that I didn't like. And don't we seek help for lots of things with life – a plumber to fix a leak, a plasterer to fix a crack, a dentist to fix a broken tooth? Why would I not talk to an expert in work about something I would be doing for another fifty years? It was my husband who made the decision for me. He gave me a necessary ultimatum: you have to change your career, or you have to find a way to live with it. He had been witness to a hundred moans. My dissatisfaction was not just mine, it was his, too.

I made the phone call.

My initial goal when meeting with Susie was a pretty lofty one: I wanted to know what I should do with my life. I am not sure if I ever worked that out, but here are three things that I did learn.

1 – What does work mean to me?

I needed to address what I meant when I talked about work. I had always considered work separate to life, that the former funded the latter. I had understood that the contract we made with the world was that we would sacrifice large portions of our time in order to make the money that we would use in our retirement for the things we really loved doing. I had to unpick three decades of conditioning that had taught me that work couldn't be enjoyable.

Working with Susie made me ask myself, *what if work and life could coexist?* Such a thing seemed possible if you found joy in your work. There is a saying that if you do what you love, you'll never work a day in your life. I am not sure that's entirely true, but I began to see there was something in the idea that if you can build a career around something that you care about, whether that's the arts, or sciences, or sport – even the hard stuff feels worth doing. I had imagined that my life would be working for forty years until I could retire and enjoy the fruits of my labour, but if you so enjoyed your work that retirement was, in fact, something to be avoided. If your work matched your interests, this all seemed possible.

I also learned the term "portfolio career". I had never considered that a person might have more than one job. The instability of such a concept worried me, but I came to see that this could be a way of offering more stability: should one area fail, I would have other areas to fall back on.

Susie asked me to list the different aspects of work that were important to me: that it should be beneficial to society, that it should be somehow creative, that it should give me a certain standard of living, that I could work both alone and with others, that I could build expertise. What if, Susie said, you took on different jobs to fulfil different needs? I didn't, then, necessarily need to 'choose' a career, I could develop several, different projects that kept me fulfilled in different ways.

2 – Short-term pain for long-term gain

A major sticking point for me was the ongoing anxiety around stability. I was very afraid of losing a regular income and of being in precarious work, and this fear was holding me back. I also felt anxious about relying on my husband's income fully or partially for a period of time. Though I don't think this way now, at the time it felt "unfeminist": relying on a man went against everything I had been taught about being independent in womanhood. But, a committed relationship is about working as a team, and one partner supporting the other through a change, regardless of gender, should be normalised and not seen as a loss of independence, but an investment in the family unit.

I talked through these anxieties about income with Susie, and she shared a thought: would a stable career in a field I cared about be worth two or three years of financial uncertainty? Because, if I worked towards a career goal I was truly passionate about I would, eventually, generate a stable income from it. The choice before me was not to leave financial stability for a lifetime, just for the time it took to become what I wanted to be. I needed to take short-term losses for long-term gains. This changed my outlook. It made a jump into a portfolio style career feel less like a jump into the unknown, but a step on a pathway to a goal.

3 – With great risk comes great reward

In one of our sessions, Susie gave me an exercise. I drew a horizontal line, left to right, on a piece of paper. Above the line would be lifetime high points, below would be low points. I was to draw dots on the page to identify those moments in my life that had been good and bad. Then, I drew a line connecting the dots to make a sort of line graph of my life. Finally, Susie asked me to annotate the graph with stars for points where I made a risky decision.

When I was finished, I put the piece of paper on the table between us. What patterns could I see? It was abundantly clear. Risky decisions led to high points in my life. The decision to leave my first job to go travelling, despite being on the fast track to a senior role; the decision to return to university for a Master's degree. I could also see in the absence of high points those times when I had resisted taking a risk: the many times I decided against quitting my first degree; the time I didn't apply for a creative writing course. High risks come with high rewards, sticking to safety led to missed opportunities. What could I achieve if I took a risk now? What would my graph look like in another ten years, if stayed as I was?

It is interesting to me now, that in reflecting on the experience of addressing my conceptions about work, and challenging my resistance to risk, I take an analytical view. I feel able to assess the way I felt and the actions I took in an almost clinical way. At the time, I know that I felt deeply emotional about the situation in which I found myself, and intensely sad at what I thought was time wasted through years of forcing myself into a box that would not accommodate my shape. That I can view these feelings and the contexts in which they arose as if from a distance is perhaps a reflection of how far I have journeyed in my understanding of what work is, and how it intersects with life. But this analytical approach to problem solving has been, perhaps, a blessing and curse in my professional life. It has helped me navigate difficult situations by employing hard armour, and cutting through emotions to their central causes. But it has perhaps also made me deaf to the messages that I have sent myself. By separating emotion from decision making, I have perhaps ignored signs that I have been unhappy because – according to all that I have learned – there was no central cause for that unhappiness. I had work, good pay, a social life. I saw my unhappiness and dissatisfaction, perhaps, as a fault in me rather than a symptom of a bigger issue. It is worth remembering that emotions are also important data in decision making.

All of these revelations were helping me to build a case for myself that it was time to leave my job, and try something new. But none of these realisations could tell me what the something new should be. It was all very well talking about creating passion projects, and working in areas of interest, but what were they? We looked at different roles: strategy roles, communications roles in different industries. They were all fine, but they didn't capture my imagination. There was only one thing that I had consistently loved, a thing I had happily poured hours into without reward or expectation. It was storytelling, or more specifically, writing stories. What if, Susie said, you became a writer?

It seemed absurd. People didn't just *become* writers. But a seed was planted. I began to research. Was it possible, could you plan a career in writing?

The answer that came back from the internet was, in short, no. Becoming a poet or a novelist or a playwright required years of hard graft. You needed of course to be talented, and you needed to write something (or many things) without any kind of reward, then you needed to be picked up by an agent, and even then, most writers didn't earn enough to live solely through writing. There would be no job posting for 'novelist', no interview, no career path. But what if I began to write, seriously write. What if I began to act as if – no matter how unlikely – I wanted that to be my career. What then?

Suddenly, I had a goal. A far-off goal, a goal most people don't ever reach, but a goal nonetheless. I could begin to build a working life around this plan. I began to research creative writing courses, applied for one and was accepted. I researched sabbaticals in my workplace, to see if I could take a year out to write – it was possible. I began to wonder if I should stay in my job at all: what if I quit, set myself up as a freelancer, and created a flexible workday that allowed me more time for my novel?

And just like that, I was unstuck.

It meant redefining what work was meant to be. It meant financial instability. It meant spending money on education, and setting myself up in a business. It meant, in short, risk.

It has been nearly two years since I handed in my notice. Am I a novelist yet? I am not. Am I happier – a hundred times over. I earn more freelancing than I did in full-time, salaried roles. I can pick and choose the paid science writing work I take on and set my own, flexible hours that leave me the time to work on my creative writing. There is a new satisfaction, too, in my freelance work that I couldn't find in salaried roles. Now I can see clearly the line from the rewards I receive each month to the work that I do. Now each project I work on with a client has a beginning and an end, and at their close I feel satisfied, as if I have reached a goal. It's not my dream job, but it's much closer to that work-life integration that I hope to achieve.

And as for my writing, I continue to work on my book. Every morning I sit at my desk and write page by page. I may never achieve a traditional ideal of success with my writing but that is the risk I have signed up for. The biggest risk of all: to imagine what could be possible.

CHAPTER TWO

Being Brave

A RESPONSE TO ANGELA FROM SUSIE

> Everyone has talent. What's rare is the courage to follow it to the dark places where it leads.
>
> Erica Jong

Why is courage a topic for this book? We assume courage has to be about knights slaying dragons or maybe a Russian opposition leader being prepared to be imprisoned for their beliefs. We witness a small teenage girl addressing the United Nations on the subject of climate change.

But as you read the stories in this book you will discover many moving examples of everyday courage in working lives. Angela decides to resign from her secure, evolving career in communications to write a novel. She wonders why it has taken her so long. We have a sense that these writers have made a choice to embrace and deeply participate in their lives. As our career paths become more fluid and we have increasingly high expectations from our work, it can feel like there is real necessity and desire to make change happen. But for many of us, this brings deep discomfort.

The dictionary tells us that courage can be defined as 'the quality of mind or spirit that enables a person to face difficulty, danger, pain, etc., without fear; bravery.' David Whyte (i), the poet, has a more profound explanation: 'To be courageous is not necessarily to go anywhere or do anything except to make conscious those things we already feel deeply and then to live through the unending vulnerabilities of those consequences.'

Courage is a decision; freedom lies in being bold

Courage is about moving away from the familiar, the tried and tested. It's about, as the title of a classic self-help book by Susan Jeffers (ii), identified, 'feeling the fear'and doing it anyway. That sounds pretty straightforward, doesn't it? But of course, there are many barriers to 'doing it anyway'. We experience this fear in both our mind and our body. My client, Sanjay, describes the maelstrom of emotions in a more specific way when embarking on a career change interview: 'I recognise this instinctive feeling of panic and doubt. As is often the case, my head assumes and favours the potential negative energy with little consideration that it could be something more optimistic. My impostor syndrome believes that my industry knowledge won't hold up if they ask for specifics in any way (beyond personal experience), and this feeling that I have 'lied' to them about the numbers – it's the awkwardness in the silent pause or fumbling of my words. And this feeling that they'll want to challenge me and catch me out for some reason.'

When we want to do something differently, we instinctively want to construct a plan. We move into action mode. We search for our CV, often applying aimlessly for roles. Wise twentieth-century career advice focused on building self-understanding and then designing a course of action. A single plan built through careful analysis. This might have been effective when the working landscape was more clearly delineated but a different approach is now called for. This traditional approach assumed that we have one 'self' and once we unearth it, off we go. A more experimental approach now seems more relevant. Hermina Ibarra of London Business School in her book, *Working Identity* (iii), explores how we are experimenting with multiple selves and identities and it is by doing and experimenting that we discover where we fit, where we will thrive.

But where do we start? And if we are fearful how do we even begin this process? My client, Harry, applies himself assiduously to thinking about what drives him now, building a powerful career story, exploring dimensions of his personality that have shaped his experiences and gaining clarification on his strengths. So now he can start experimenting, right? But now comes the tough bit. He tells me: 'If I have to be brutally honest, we have hit on things that I am uncomfortable with, which makes me reluctant to move forward. The harsh reality is that in the last nine years my career does not have that many highlights and I am struggling how to portray myself as a result of that. My confidence levels are also still quite low.'

There is a real tension between the reflection part of the career change process and the subsequent action part. The difficult truth is that we can never be fully prepared for change, we must acknowledge the discomfort and take some small steps to doing things differently. Brené Brown, the American academic (iv), has written wisely on the topic of vulnerability. She explains brilliantly: 'Vulnerability is not winning or losing; it's having the courage to show up when you can't control the outcome.'

The woman on top of the mountain didn't fall there

My client, Jane, had been at her organisation for fourteen years and had outgrown her role. Her agenda for coaching was to finally make a move. She was reluctant to apply for promotion or explore opportunities externally. She was aware of the strategy: 'Making changes must come from action. I need to take action. I can practise and take risks. One thing I always knew ... but was reinforced ... is that only I can make the changes and I must be braver!' Sadly, Jane is still in the same role, in the same organisation.

So what is the secret? Why do some people find change so tough even when they so desire it? It might actually be easier when life events seem to propel you to change; it can feel as though you have no choice.

It's spring 2008. I have a rewarding job in a prestigious London university, I am newly divorced, supporting three young daughters. I am at the top of the salary scale and that salary won't be enough to keep us in the style to which we are accustomed, in fact, not much style at all. Action is required and I decide to resign to start my own consultancy. Superficially this might look pretty courageous but at the time it felt like the 'sensible' option, even as if I had no choice. Looking back, it's been a truly wonderful and rich adventure and I have learnt so much, just by 'going for it' and experimenting with all the opportunities that have come my way.

Of course that isn't the only story, there have been many challenges.

Jim was one of the two founding partners of a private equity company. Aged forty, he was immersed in deal making, running a company and enjoying the financial rewards that his work had brought. Then he tragically lost his wife to breast cancer. This resulted in a profound rethink of his priorities and values and he left this work behind. Twenty years later he has steered a charity working with disengaged young people into a successful merger and now has founded an organisation focused on speeding up government action for a healthy planet.

Most of us potter on, wrapped up in parenthood and/or the challenges of sustaining a living. We might have small intimations that our work is not as fulfilling as we hoped, but we focus on our day to day. Disaster hasn't struck; we are "making do" but with a sense that there might be something more. Making change happen feels too uncomfortable and we remind ourselves how "lucky" we really are. The pandemic challenged many of us in multiple ways, losing those we love and glimpsing intimations of our own mortality. We might have reflected more on what we really want and care about but simultaneously our anxiousness around making change connects us back to that very primal sense of vulnerability. We want to anticipate and control everything around us.

REFLECT

Take a piece of paper and try to answer the questions below. Set a timer for 15 minutes.
Return to this exercise over a couple of weeks. It will help turn abstract ideas into specifics.

→ What do I really, really want?

→ Things would have been much better had I …

→ What am I tolerating/putting up with?

→ What didn't I do that I could have done?

→ The feelings and emotions I am noticing …

→ If there was nothing holding me back, the things I would be trying out are …

So what does courageous career change look and feel like? We know that it could be something to do with connecting with what you really want now. What have you learnt in the light of new experiences? What has shifted for you? The idea is to acknowledge and not deny the feelings of fear and doubt, but also take steps to move towards your goals. Fear and panic are really powerful emotions, but they're not ones that we want to do away with. They evolved to help us as a species to survive, to protect ourselves. While we shouldn't push them away, we also shouldn't let them take over our lives. Instead of letting them own us, we should remember we own them. You have permission to be afraid while taking steps to change your career path, but don't let that fear paralyse you into inaction. You can take baby steps to build your courage "muscle".

Take a look at how my client, Sarah, began to map out her future possibilities and experiments:

STRENGTHS - ABILITY
- CAN ACCEPT A CHALLENGE
- INTUITIVE
- UNCONVENTIONAL
- RELIABLE
- A STRONG SET OF PRINCIPLES
- I KNOW WHEN TO TALK UP OR TALK DOWN
- IMAGINATIVE
- ENTHUSIASTIC
- PERSONABLE, PERCEPTIVE
- PERSUASIVE & VERSATILE

PLAN

VALUES
- MAKING LIFE A JOYOUS ONE
- LISTENING
- KINDNESS
- APPRECIATION OF BEAUTY
- INDIVIDUALITY

CREATIVITY
- PAINTING
- PHOTO COLLAGE
- AS ART ABOVE

ART
- DEVOTING MY TIME TO CREATIVITY
- A BODY OF WORK:
  - A GALLERY - EXHIBITIONS &
  - A PORTFOLIO OF ILLUSTRATIONS FOR PUBLICATION

COMEDY/ACTING
- TRYING TO GAIN REPRESENTATION FOR COMEDY ACTING
- CREATING & WRITING A COMEDY SHOW
- STAND UP

ENTREPRENEURIAL
- SETTING UP A BUSINESS
- A GALLERY (POSSIBLE CAR TOO)
- OBJECTS
- POP UP RESTAURANT
- CAR BOOT / VINTAGE

THERAPEUTIC
- TRAINING TO BE A PSYCHOTHERAPIST - THERAPY IN COMPANY COACHING

CREATIVITY

CAREER EQUATION

DOING SOMETHING WITH CREATIVITY AND TRUE MEANING AND VALUE

FINANCIAL SECURITY

INTELLECTUAL
- HR - AGENDA - STUDYING HUMAN BEHAVIOUR - THERAPY
- ART PRO. COORDINATOR ONLINE

REALITY
JOY & GRATITUDE

MAIN VALUES AND PRIORITIES
- GOOD SALARY / MONEY
- GROWING & BEING STIMULATED
- CREATIVITY & INDIVIDUALISM
- WORKING WITH LIKE MINDED AND INSPIRATIONAL PEOPLE

COMBINATION MACHINE

TEST

PART TIME JOB
BRINGING GOOD MONEY (USING THIS IN WITH -CREATIVE PROJECTS AND THERAPEUTIC ENVIRONMENT.

CAREER ELEMENT

TRAINING TO BE A THERAPIST:
- TO HELP AND ALLOW PEOPLE TO TALK
- FOR PERSONAL GROWTH
- FOR CREATIVE STUDY

THERAPEUTIC

CREATING / WORKING ON A CREATIVE PROJECT FOR GALLERY SHOW / BOOK PUBLICATIONS / CHILDREN'S ROOMS

CREATIVITY

ART

CURATING

WRITING
- CHILDREN'S STORIES
- SCRIPT
- SHORT STORIES (UNFINISHED)

CURATING
- TRAINING TO WORK IN A GALLERY
- MANAGING SMALL SPACE → LARGER

INTERIORS/ CHILDREN'S ROOMS

OPERATIONS
- JOB SEARCH FOR SIMILAR ROLES IN A BETTER ENVIRONMENT WITH BETTER CAREER SUPPORT

PEOPLE / TEAM MANAGEMENT
- SIMILAR ROLE BUT PARTLY TEACHING OR PEOPLE AND TEAM BUILDING

STRATEGIC
- CONTINUING CAREER IN BUSINESS
- DEVELOPING SKILLS

CAREER
- DIRECTOR OF ...
- HEAD OF ...
- RUNNING A TEAM OVERSEEING

WHICH INDUSTRIES?

CONSIDERATIONS
- FINANCIAL FAMILY OBLIGATIONS
- I NEED TO EARN MONEY TO CONTRIBUTE TO THE BUILDING WORKS
- NOT POSSIBLE TO SPEND MONTHS REDESIGNING

Not REALLY CALLING FOR IT / HOLDING?

TRUST TERRIFYING

I COULD DO IT

WANT TO DO THIS THE MOST

FINANCIAL SECURITY

NO FINANCIAL SECURITY / DIFFICULT TO MAKE MONEY

FEELS RIGHT / WOULD LOVE TO DO THIS

GOOD, BUT MAYBE NOT REALLY STRETCHING (BUT THIS IS A REALITY AND AFTER ALL)

We think of courage purely as facing up to our fears. But it is also deeply connected with profound beliefs about who we are, who we want to be, who we love and what we wish the world could be. Psychoanalyst Erik Erikson (v), described our development as epigenetic; we are growing outwards around the edges of our younger selves. It's about acknowledging our past and understanding what we carry from it. Angela tells us that she had to let go of her parents' perception that work was hard graft, not to be enjoyed. This belief exerted a powerful presence that affected her decisions and distorted her perceptions.

The psychologist Albert Bandura (vi), explored the concept of self-efficacy. How do we build a sense that we can make things happen? How much confidence do we have in our ability to exert control over our motivation, our behaviour and our environment? My client, Jane, explores how to build self-efficacy through experience, through trying to build some mastery: 'I had a discussion with my staff member currently working on the project. I gave him some feedback and praise about his great work. It always feels uncomfortable to see the embarrassed silence that follows. In addition, part of me still feels not qualified to give this kind of feedback. We also discussed his move to the new project. Definitely went well. Still nervous on how to make it happen in detail.'

We have to do stuff to build this sense of being able to effect change. We can often feel isolated when reimagining our working identity; we have to walk this path alone and we believe that this might cause short-term pain to those around us. Arianna explains: 'If I resign from my dull but reliable long-term role, I will lose my steady income and my routine which easily enables me to be a mother. Paradoxically, I have energy and a curiosity to change, but I am also fundamentally afraid of it at the same time.' Arianna knows what she wants: 'Less of an office mentality, trying to fit into an ideal that is not making me happy and more of starting to create again and quiet time for reflection and solitude.

REFLECT   Tips for building courage

Observe people around you; seeing others succeed through their hard work increases our belief that we can master something

Re-frame fear as something that happens when you push the boundaries; the butterflies in your stomach are excitement and you might keep feeling them but it's a sign of doing something new not a weakness

Reflect on a time when you have been courageous; taking a moment to think about your strengths and achievements can build courage

Acknowledge and reward great questions and instances of "I don't know, but I'd like to find out" as daring leadership behaviours. The big shift here is from wanting to "be right" to wanting to "get it right."

Life is messy and non linear

We want our lives to be "perfect", to live up to some glossy ideal of how things should be and this can hold us back from making courageous steps as we fear failing. What does it mean to live courageously in a world where all our passions and projects might not succeed as we want them to? The French psychoanalyst and philosopher, Anne Dufourmantelle (vii), argues that risk is an inherent part of living fully in the world. Risk-free living, she argues, is not living at all. Courage is as much about living, despite knowing the exposed nerve of love and passion could trigger chest-tightening pain at any moment. Yet so often we close ourselves from the world to keep ourselves safe. We tell ourselves stories in the shower, imagining all the things we could do – could be – if only the world would let us. Take a look at chapter twenty-one on perfectionism and procrastination.

A call to action for all of us, then. How can we have the courage to experiment, take small steps and discover where they might lead?

CHAPTER THREE

The Big 3-0

SEAN

Writing about my career just six months shy of turning the big 3-0 should come naturally enough. I've spent the past few weeks – months maybe – thinking about little else. My love-hate relationship with my work as a brand consultant has come to dominate my home life, my headspace, and kept me up many a night as I've made my way through my twenties.

Whilst my imminent birthday is an arbitrary milestone, it nonetheless feels like a good point to pull over, stop, and really think about the direction I'm heading in. In fact, as I've been reflecting and writing this piece, I've decided once and for all to quit my job as a brand consultant, and instead apply to a social innovation programme: taking my "career" in a totally different direction. Perhaps turning thirty won't turn out to be so arbitrary after all?

Making big changes whilst I still can – no kids, no mortgage – feels vital to building both a meaningful career, and living a life in pursuit of something bigger than just financial security. I've long felt the calling of a more purposeful career … Whilst I have loved working in the creative sector, I have realised my own values are poorly aligned with the revenue-hungry agencies I have chosen to work in. It's been an eye-opening experience to work with clients that range from the Mayor of London to global med-tech companies, but as my experience has grown, the nagging sense of dissatisfaction has become harder to ignore.

I know for certain when the cracks first started to appear. The suicide of one of my best friends, Josh, forced me to acknowledge the disconnect between our surface-level 'work selves' and the emotional chaos that lay hidden just beneath. This happened early in my career, but the uncomfortable truths I had to face up to have only crystallised with time.

Whilst Josh's story is too complicated to try and unpack here, reflecting on our friendship and parallel experiences – both in work and outside of it – has helped me make some sense of the emotional journey that has led me to where I am today. Anyone who has experienced the grief and trauma of someone being torn out of your life so suddenly will understand that subsequent numbness; the disconnect between your reality and everyone else's, and how it leads you to question things in a way that perhaps some people are lucky enough not to have to.

Growing up, Josh and I had spent many a bus trip to college plotting our futures – first, which universities we'd apply to, and later, where we saw ourselves in our thirties, forties and so on. A pair of headstrong teenagers, the future at that point seemed so bright and undaunting.

In the immediate aftermath of Josh's death I used work to pave over the emotions I was experiencing. Whatever early doubts I'd had about my choice of profession, I now firmly shut them out, filling my time with reassuringly bland and repetitive tasks like budget reconciliations and presentation formatting. As my world inside crumbled and my emotions longed to escape, my brain imprisoned those thoughts and feelings in spreadsheets, powerpoints, emails and timelines.

Sometimes my 'true self' would still shine through and I would wheel out the 1000-megawatt Sean for client presentations, workshops and pitches. But, as soon as these performances were over, it was straight back to autopilot. Around this time I also became distant and withdrawn in my personal life, and irrevocably convinced that my professional relationships were hollow and inauthentic.

The last time I really remember feeling alive, present and kicking is when I first applied to a graduate role at The Value Engineers, back in 2014. I'd always looked on marketing as something of a 'dark art', but a fortuitous conversation with one of TVE's typically brainy and charismatic consultants, Martha, persuaded me to give brand consulting a shot.

I had already begun to develop a nascent interest in branding and innovation, having started a social enterprise crowdsourcing Caribbean food products from the local community in Hackney. The flavours, family histories and, above all, the people I connected with remain some of the most life-changing experiences I've ever had.

At one point it looked like we were set to open a restaurant moments away from Dalston Junction, whilst simultaneously holding discussions with Waitrose. However it was precisely these opportunities that highlighted the fact that I had neither the team, experience or skillset necessary to execute them.

Joining The Value Engineers, I told myself, was an opportunity to strengthen my commercial knowledge, really getting under the skin of how brands are built, and working with some of the world's leading food and drink brands. I would then bring this experience back into the world of social enterprise, and perhaps even pick up where I'd left off a couple of years down the line.

The experience quickly stacked up: running workshops helping the likes of Strongbow, McDonalds, Nestlé and Müller to launch new products and campaigns. As my consulting experience grew, however, the idea of giving up a monthly pay cheque became ever more daunting.

Reflecting back now, I am struck by how much my decisions have been driven by financial incentives instead of more intrinsic motivations. Whilst many of my friends and peers went on to study for a Masters, my parents had drilled it into me that the overarching goal was to secure a stable and well-paying job.

There's no question my parents instilled a hunger for learning in me from a young age, but when it came to university their own experiences were vastly limited. Having both left the education system at 16, financial self sufficiency was the bedrock of my parents' values. This left me in a strange limbo as the first in my family to go to university, but also at odds with many of my more middle-class classmates who saw academia as an end goal, just as much a means.

Having grown up with next to nothing, my dad has always placed great emphasis on money: not just as a source of stability, but at times as a substitute for intimacy or affection also. Whilst more generous with her emotions, my mum has long had a habit of squirrelling away any money she gets her hands on, avoids talking about it religiously, and taught us from a very young age how frozen peas and tinned sweetcorn could be used to "bulk out" just about any meal you can think of.

It is only now, after seven years of hard work and scrupulous savings, that I am finally beginning to challenge the beliefs instilled in me by my parents, and re-examine the role that money plays in my life. This re-examination is partly driven by necessity (I am still a long way off being able to afford a home in London), but predominantly through my desire to live a meaningful life, unconstrained by the anxieties that money imposes on us.

Self-sufficiency as a core value is by no means a bad starting point; after all what is being an adult if not the ability to stand on your own two feet and live off the money you've gone out and earned yourself? But as I have learned more about economics, investing and pensions (my favourite rabbit hole to disappear down), the constraints of my family's working-class attitudes toward money and risk have become clearer.

Looking at how this has impacted my career choices, it seems I've always placed financial security and earning potential ahead of more abstract concepts such as "happiness" and "fulfillment".

Surprisingly, it was never one of my childhood dreams to become a corporate brand consultant. Instead, at a very young age I was busy dreaming of becoming an archaeologist. I still remember the intimidating journey to a Year Six classroom to find a dictionary that spelled out my early choice of career. At some point my interest in pyramids and pharaohs shifted towards snakes, lizards and and the field of herpetology: studying reptiles. Every page of my illustrated encyclopedia and every new programme on TV or book I borrowed from the library led to a new life of adventure; the more esoteric, the more alluring.

I came surprisingly (uncomfortably?) close to the working world of herpetologists whilst working for my dad one summer, between university terms. We'd sold a CCTV system to 'Crocodiles of the World' and during the install I got to see these magnificently menacing reptiles up close and personal. By that point, however, my career ambitions had moved on several pages in the encyclopedia.

It was when I started to get closer to choosing my A levels that my interests began to coalesce. After much time and consideration I decided what I really wanted was to become a psychologist. I read voraciously about personality disorders, how children's brains develop, and how we process our emotions. I sifted through university prospectuses and wondered if I was destined to end up working in a school, a prison, a private practice or a psychiatric institution.

Hoewever, one fateful day, I stumbled across a totally unrepresentative careers page on prospects.ac.uk that said the highest salary an experienced psychologist might ever command was in the £40-60,000 region. That was it. Just like that my interest in becoming a psychologist evaporated. I knew my parents would be proud and support me, whatever career path I chose, but there was no way could I justify having chosen a career with such an arbitrary earning cap.

Several years later I've learned the hard way that our time is far more valuable than even the most generous of pay cheques. There is so much in life – love, adventure, growth, connection, and feeling like what you do matters – that can't be measured by the numbers on your pay cheque. This is a big reason I've taken to get off the hamster wheel mid-career, and ensure I spend my thirties and beyond in pursuit of something more meaningful.

Getting to this point, however, has been a journey. From the very first time my parents joked they would kick me out at sixteen to make my own way, to their recent anxieties about me quitting my job and throwing away my financial security, I have had to find a balance between the values that shaped me, and the vision that will take me forward.

My parents themselves have made huge progress: from working in the warehouse where they met, to living next door to a lake in the Cotswolds. For them, hard work and an aversion to risk has helped them build a better life for their family. For me, however, there is a wider world to explore, risks worth taking, and goals more important than making money.

To invoke an old cliché though, the apple really doesn't fall that far from the tree. My dad would never use the word, but he is an entrepreneur, having started his own business in the midst of the 2008 recession. In contrast, my mum was a social worker with the NSPCC for a long time, and it's from her I inherit a sense of social responsibility, and an almost moral obligation to help others get ahead.

It is perhaps not surprising, then, that I find myself seeking a "middle way" that balances purpose and profit; a career path that enables me to be my own boss, help people, and still make money, but with a bigger appetite to drive positive change in the world.

A healthy scepticism towards authority is another character trait instilled by my parents. Playing out with mixed results, I've always believed authority is there to be questioned and challenged – respected subject to results, not on status alone.

I remember one particularly formative moment when we found out my dad would be leaving his job to start his own business, around the time I was revising for my GCSE exams. The story, as it was relayed to us, was that Dad had closed a significant six-figure deal, cementing his reputation as the company's most valuable salesman. He'd returned triumphant to the office, expecting his company car upgrade to be hastened through, only to be rewarded with a remote-control helicopter (some sort of executive toy) but denied the company car he coveted. It was at that point my dad achieved mythical status among his soon-to-be-ex colleagues by telling his bosses to go f**k themselves and essentially handed his notice in on the spot.

I recount this tale, not to glorify my dad's behaviour, but to give a bit of context to where my own attitudes towards authority come from, or more accurately my inability to suffer fools gladly. Time has confirmed dad's decision as a good one: leaving behind his company car aspirations he went on to start his own business in the midst of the 2008 recession, setting himself and my mum up for early retirement after a decade of hard work.

My own skirmishes with authority, however, have burned out a series of bosses: something I am rather less proud of than my dad's spectacular act of defiance. Vocal back and forth 'debates' with my first boss led to our then managing director asking us to keep the noise down because, whilst she knew we weren't trying to kill each other, she was getting tired of reassuring other people in the building this was the case. Seeing him at a book launch a few months after I left sent my pulse sky-rocketing, and gave me an insight into how unhealthy that way of working must have been for us both.

Fortunately the agency I subsequently found myself in saw potential underneath the constant questioning and headstrong nature. Perhaps also sensing there was something deeper to this emotional turbulence, they decided to invest in a series of leadership coaching sessions with Susie. Whilst Susie was clear about the differences between coaching and therapy from the get go, the opportunities for reflection, with the guide of an experienced coach and workplace psychologist, were invaluable to my personal growth. Susie's focus on authenticity, and quality of mission continue to guide me, even as my career path diverges from where our paths first crossed.

One particular exchange to which I keep returning was triggered by a seemingly innocent question when we first met. In the swanky surroundings of Covent Garden's H Club, Susie had enquired what my parents did for a living. 'I don't see how that's relevant,' I shot back with unwarranted venom at the time. Clearly whatever chip I had on my shoulder about my rough-around-the-edges parents and working-class upbringing was clouding the fact that Susie was simply trying to initiate a conversation about the attitudes and ingrained beliefs I bring to the workplace. Of course, now I can look back at that exchange with much greater clarity (assisted in no small part by Susie's coaching and insights), but more importantly I can see how my parents' attitudes towards work, their unrelenting emotional honesty, and willingness to forge their own paths have both shaped my values, and played out as key themes in my own career.

Another good example of this is the fact that my mum's "career" for most of our childhoods was working as a childminder – enabling her to be a stay-at-home mum for my sister and me in exchange for dividing her attention among a rotating cast of several other children.

When you grow up as an assistant childminder to your mum, it's all hands on deck – an early apprenticeship (unpaid of course) and one which has stayed with me years later. Working with clients across a range of different corporate environments, I never cease to be amazed when I observe many of the same attention-seeking and resource-maximising behaviours I saw modelled by childminder kids all those years ago.

We are quick to dismiss many such behaviours as office politics and "playing the game", but I have often found it insightful to observe how they reveal people's deeper motivations, and highlight the contrast between the surface level "work self" we present to the world, and the more evasive self which is often hidden away behind that mask.

This divided self can arise as a self-defence or coping mechanism, but I think evidences a dangerous disconnect in our workplaces. It's no coincidence that even as my friend Josh's personal life collapsed into chaos, he continued to show up to work as the sharp-suited ambitious graduate they'd hired, instead of reaching out for the help he needed.

I believe that if we can't apply our full selves to our work, then chances are we're not working in the right place. This doesn't mean doing away with diplomacy, dismissing other people's way of doing things, or ignoring opportunities to grow and change. What it does mean is that our emotions, our inner child, and that bubbling chaos of energy and imagination within all of us are there waiting to be channelled, but we need the right structure, environments and colleagues to help us tap into our authentic selves.

For me, this means leaving a stable job and a predictable (but rewarding) career path, in pursuit of life experiences that are better aligned with my values. These are the values forged by my childhood, my parents, and the background I come from. They're also grounded in the backstory and experiences I spent most of my late teens and entire twenties trying to run away from.

As my financial situation has become more secure and my

material surroundings more comfortable, I have felt my inner life become increasingly bereft. Likewise my tenure and reliability in the workplace have led to a plateau professionally. Despite this, the generous increases in my salary and the move to a four-day week has – to this point – taken precedence over the urge to escape and find new challenges and opportunities to grow.

I've loved being a brand consultant, and peering into the lives and workplaces of surgeons, insurance brokers, woundcare nurses, and brand managers. The skills I've learned, the designers I've collaborated with, and the mentors I've met along the way will always underpin how I approach new situations. That's the beauty of experience – it's not something you lose or leave behind, unless you're too busy to appreciate how much it influences how you operate.

The reason I'm leaving the career I've loved is, ultimately, because the impact of even the most insightful PowerPoint presentation can never measure up to the emotional realities and life experiences of people who exist outside of the corporate bubble. The temptation for the past few years has been to gradually give in to the "a job is a job" mindset, and instead seek fulfilment elsewhere – in my personal life, my hobbies (if I had any), and/or my holidays. But for me that is the difference between a job and a career – one you do for income, the other is your vehicle for contributing to the world around you.

Depending on your perspective as a reader, this impulse to diverge from the 'career path' I've been on for the past seven years may sound equal parts brave, foolish, naïve, optimistic or misguided. Maybe seven years sounds like a lot to throw away, maybe it's the best decision I'll ever make. It undoubtedly has tones of being a premature mid-life crisis, but opening myself up to a little chaos now is also clearing the ground for future growth. The fact these things are so subjective is the wonderful thing about careers – they are not external, objective and separate from us ... they are us!"

In spite of constant talk of 'climbing the ladder" and "getting ahead", in recent years I've really come to terms with the fact there is no great scoreboard in the sky. No one is keeping count. Being a doctor, lawyer or architect is truly admirable for the work it entails, and the capacity to impact people's lives, but beyond the dinner party small talk I am interested in people who have found careers where they can be truly authentic – and whilst my bank balance might not thank me, that's the kind of person I aspire to become as I step into my next decade.

CHAPTER FOUR

Why Do We Work?

A RESPONSE TO SEAN FROM SUSIE

> Life is never made unbearable by circumstances, but only by lack of meaning and purpose.
>
> Victor Frankel

Sean contrasts his perspectives on what work should mean with those held by his parents. Like him we are often constrained by the messages handed down to us by our communities. When I worked with Sean, he was beginning to challenge his long-held beliefs about work, status and money. He felt a glimmer of possibility; might he allow himself to step away and train to work as a social entrepreneur? Fast forward to 2023 and Sean has completed this training and is setting up his own social impact brand consultancy.

Until the mid-twentieth century the majority of the global population saw work purely as a means to an end and of course it still is for many across the globe today. But over recent decades, work and career have become central to how we see ourselves and evaluate our fulfillment. Those wise thinkers from over two millennia ago understood the nuanced relationship between enjoyment and work. Aristotle (i) simply declared: 'Pleasure in the job puts perfection in the work.'

We can recourse to the Ancient Greeks again for their wonderful definition, Eudaimonia. Eudaimonia means achieving the optimum conditions possible for a human being, not only happiness, but also virtue, morality, and a meaningful life. We have a sense that work can be one way of fulfilling our unique potential as a human being.

Don't let anyone else hold the pen

But what does finding meaning and purpose at work really mean and how do you acquire it? Here is the challenge; it's tough! Finding meaning and purpose isn't about the pursuit of hedonism, it's about understanding what interests and motivates you and then working through the difficult times. It's about accessing something more valuable than happiness, a sense that we have made a difference. It's about beliefs and behaviour that you cherish and give you a sense of meaning and satisfaction.

My client, Sam, writes about his quest for meaning: 'I want to really understand what kind of environment I thrive in. I have a vague idea of this, but tend to forget and repeat old patterns. We understand that what will give us meaning will be hard to develop.'

This is Sam's very high-level shopping list for purpose:

1. Being more integral in an organisation
2. Valuing myself more
3. Stopping numbing my fears
4. Collaborating with people

What might your shopping list look like?

It's useful to distinguish here between the more universal aspects of being human that are important to all of us and what you as an individual find uniquely meaningful. Many of us are familiar with Maslow's hierarchy of needs (see table below) (ii). The majority of us in affluent societies have lives in which Maslow's first two levels are no longer a real issue. What do humans need when their survival and safety is assured? Maslow's other three levels, belonging, esteem and self-actualisation, were attempts to answer this question.

Maslow's Hierarchy of Needs

1. **Physiological needs:** These most basic human survival needs include food and water, sufficient rest, clothing and shelter, overall health, and reproduction. Maslow states that these basic physiological needs must be addressed before humans move on to the next level of fulfillment.

2. **Safety needs:** Safety needs include protection from violence and theft, emotional stability and well-being, health security, and financial security.

3. **Love and belonging needs:** The social needs on the third level of Maslow's hierarchy relate to human interaction and are the last of the so-called lower needs. Among these needs are friendships and family bonds – both with biological family and chosen family. Physical and emotional intimacy ranging from sexual relationships to intimate emotional bonds are important to achieving a feeling of elevated kinship. Additionally, membership in social groups contributes to meeting this need.

4. **Esteem needs:** The primary elements of esteem are self-respect (the belief that you are valuable and deserving of dignity) and self-esteem (confidence in your potential for personal growth and accomplishments). Self-esteem can be broken into two types: esteem which is based on respect and acknowledgment from others, and esteem which is based on your own self-assessment. Self-confidence and independence stem from this latter type of self-esteem.

5. **Self-actualization needs:** This describes the fulfillment of your full potential as a person.

Many people feel that their work must be of benefit to society, that the mission of their work must be focused on 'changing the world'. In my experience this doesn't have to be the case; if you are doing work that is interesting to you, and you are using the best of you, this can feel incredibly meaningful. Work can feel that it matters even if the organisation you are working for does not have a profound quality of mission.

Daniel Pink (iii), American best-selling author and influential management thinker, identified three universal motivations that make skilled work feel of value. These are autonomy, mastery and purpose. According to Pink, autonomy is the desire to direct our own lives. Pink describes mastery as the desire to continually improve at something that matters. He argues that humans love 'to get better at stuff' – they enjoy the satisfaction from personal achievement and progress. I like the idea of developing a "craft" mindset; focusing on becoming better at what you do. By doing this you develop new and rare skills and opportunities come your way. Pink describes purpose as the desire to do things in service of something larger than ourselves. Pink argues that people intrinsically want to do things that matter.

REFLECT

→What is my craft?

→What skills and strengths is this craft composed of?

→For each of these, what does 'good' look like?

→What are ways to practise these skills on a daily basis?

→What projects can I come up with to develop my craft on a daily basis?

→What is my career capital? What are my rare and valuable skills? What value can I bring?

Some of the more universal ideas already discussed might resonate with you, but how can you explore what matters to you in more depth? This goal of self-actualisation is different for each of us. Christian, another client of mine, is employed by a branding agency, working with retail clients. He writes about the meaning he gets from his work: 'I am always interested in new ideas and concepts that will create meaningful change and I enjoy challenging preconceptions to help originate new thinking.' This is when Christian feels in the flow and his work feels worthwhile.

My client, Amala, who works in education, attempts to give her values specificity: 'I have chosen three particular values, which I think demonstrate core beliefs of mine – compassionate action, creativity and development of empathy. I believe that I have a duty to prepare our students for the unknown futures and workplaces of the twenty-first century. I want to place equal importance on personal and academic development within the curriculum, and co-curricular activities. I believe in supporting ownership of development through reflection and goal setting.'

Crafting your vision

There are a number of great tools to help you to reflect on what is important to you. You might find Edgar Schein's concept of the career anchors useful (see Appendix A). A career anchor is something that changes and evolves into a dimension that shapes your working identity or self-image.

Two of Schein's anchors differentiate between finding leadership meaningful (general managerial anchor) and relishing developing an expertise in a particular speciality (technical functional anchor.) My client, Sara, explains how leadership gives her a sense of purpose: 'I am deeply interested in how to get the best out of each individual in a team, and how to organise a business best to deliver a vision. Understanding how to play the right people in the right position, what is the right organisational design for success, how to ensure everyone understands the vision in a meaningful way to them, is what makes me love leadership'.

Misha, however, is building a specialist expertise in sustainable cities: 'Being involved in journalism and photojournalism allowed me a fantastic lens (pun intended) into others' worlds. I became increasingly aware of all that I didn't know or understand. Eventually I discovered the field of urban planning, where issues of access and equity are deeply embedded, and I was immediately intrigued. My desire is to make communities more equitable for all people by focusing on challenges such as climate change, transportation, housing, and education.'

Clients enjoy drawing out a values comic strip that helps them to understand how their values have changed over their life course. Here is Julia's:

What would a world be like where we just focused on developing what we do really well? There is a strong relationship between what these strengths are and what we experience as meaningful. This is the idea that we are experiencing 'flow', a term coined by Mihaly Csikszentmihalyi (iv). At these times we feel, 'strong, alert, in effortless control, unselfconscious and at the peak of our abilities'. These sound very like Eudaimonia. As Csikszentmihalyi writes, 'The best moments in our lives are not the passive, receptive, relaxing times; the best moments usually occur if a person's body and mind is stretched to its limits in a voluntary effort to accomplish something difficult and worthwhile.'

I find Martin Seligman's VIA strengths survey useful in dissecting values (v). Below are one of my clients' top three strengths:

Top Strength – Fairness, Equity and Justice. Treating people fairly is one of your abiding principles. You do not let your personal feelings bias your decisions about other people. You give everyone a chance.

Second Strength – Curiosity and Interest in the World. You are curious about everything. You are always asking questions and you find all subjects and topics fascinating. You like exploration and discovery.

Third Strength – Bravery and Valour. You are a courageous person who does not shrink from challenge, threat, difficulty or pain. You speak up for what is right even if there is opposition, you act on your convictions.

How could my client use these strengths in his work? If he is able to, he will find his work more meaningful.

What interests you? Could this also relate to what will give you sense of meaning? Take a look at the Ten Basic Interests in chapter sixteen. It's a much more transferable way of looking at what you are curious about. Let's explore three here:

The Professor
THEORY DEVELOPMENT AND CONCEPTUAL THINKING – learning, problem solving, teaching, research, ideas, debate, imagination, theory

The Artist
CREATIVE PRODUCTION – brainstorming, creating new projects, fast pace, free thinking, loving ideas

The Coach
COUNSELLING AND MENTORING – relationships, altruism, social enterprise, teaching, counselling, psychology

I have worked with a few clients who recognised that these were their top three interests and incorporated this thinking into their career change plan. Mary, who moved from full-time teaching to starting a business supporting families as they work across the globe. Shaun, who moved from political journalism to working in a cheese shop then became a food journalist and mentor to food entrepreneurs. And Baran, who moved from strategy consultancy to academia and subsequently established her own social enterprise.

Using some of the tools mentioned above and the 'Reflect' exercises might help you to understand what is truly meaningful to you, and help you to see how your values might have changed over time. Do you have values that you have left behind? Or recognise your parents' values rather than your own? There can be tensions between some of our values; for example, we want to be a good parent but also focus on making an impact in our work. The psychologist Susan David (vi) asks: 'What if the choice was about being fully committed to both rather than being conflicted and torn?' Susan explains: 'If you say, "I value being a loving parent, I will bring that love to my interactions with my kids" and "I value being a productive worker, I will bring that productivity to my desk every day."'

Allow people to pursue their passions

Over the past few years, the "purpose-led" organisation has become a fashionable term. How can we find a place that feels like *our* place and offer something that becomes our contribution? How can we then find patterns that point to a way in which our values and interests can find a place within organisations? A value must be something we can use. We want to work in places that align with our individual sense of purpose and, if we are leading others, we want to create an environment where people can really thrive. Research shows that organisations that have an invigorating sense of purpose that goes beyond business success, and which makes people feel they are changing society, are thriving. These places have the courage to set extremely stretching goals and to be ground-breaking in the pursuit of the core purpose. They have an innovative approach to benefits and treat people in a way that makes them feel special. They also have a culture that allows people to be themselves and to feel they are personally making a difference and utilising their distinct talents. They have clear and authentically grounded values which are lived through thick and thin and a concern for the wider and, particularly, the environmental and societal impact of business activities. And through all this, they have an excellent reputation with consumers and other political and social stakeholders. Finally, they have a preparedness to sacrifice short-term gains if their achievement conflicts with the core purpose and values.

Our values are qualities of action; they are fluid and act as a guide to give us a sense of continuity and allow us to get closer to what we want in life. We have to be courageous enough to shape our choices so that we are doing what we care about; embracing the fear that we all feel when we act and behave in a novel way.

How can you use the tools I have introduced you to here to reflect on your own purpose? What conversations can you have with others to shape this thinking? What can you experiment with right now?

CHAPTER FIVE

The Less Travelled Road

GERARD

> Two roads diverged in a wood, and I – I took the one less
> travelled by, And that has made all the difference.
>
> Robert Frost

In my day-to-day job as a doctor, I often see into the lives of some of the most vulnerable in society. Often, in these cases, a combination of circumstance and poor socio-economic position can lead to tragedy. Whether it's mental illness, involvement in criminal gangs or poor physical health outcomes, there is often a point where things start to go wrong. Adolescence is usually one of those turning points. Not coming from a place of privilege myself, I understand how life can take people down difficult roads. This is why I feel so strongly about supporting people at their time of need and throughout their lives. Reflecting on my own career journey, on the forks in my own road, helps me understand the people I am called to serve.

I was lucky to be born into a loving, supportive home, but at times I felt smothered. I've lately learned that I had a difficult birth, as had my sister. This had an impact on the way my parents behaved towards us: I was loved, cossetted and "wrapped in cotton wool".

I went to a school where sporting success was always important. I wasn't sporty, so my way of succeeding was through academic achievement. I was recognised as having a good work ethic, a trait that was instilled in me by my parents from a young age. I was strongly motivated by praise. Given where I sat in my family dynamic, I was accustomed to being the centre of attention.

With my mother always worrying I would break, I evolved into an emotionally fragile teenager. I found it hard to handle the pressure of adolescence and school. Education has always been a way for people to become upwardly mobile, and this was definitely the case where I grew up. We had to do better than previous generations. My grandparents on both sides were small farmers. My father was a postman who, for lots of reasons, never completed his secondary education. My mother was a clerical officer. I had limited role models of those attending higher education, but like many people from working-class families, I felt a pressure to succeed and climb the social ladder. A lot of my early school and career decisions were heavily influenced by my parents' views and aspirations, rather than my wishes and needs.

My desire to study medicine, however, really did feel like a calling. Aged six, I had experienced the trauma of my grandfather's untimely death and the suffering and shock it engendered in my loved ones. I wonder now if part of my drive to become a doctor came from a longing to repair that rupture, stitch up that original wound. Of course, medicine also offered a respectable, stable career, which my family would approve of. What I didn't realise, at 17, when I started my career journey, was the commitment and strength it required, and the pressure that was inherent in following my calling.

Looking back now, I understand that this pressure was just too much for an emotionally fragile and insecure teenage boy. As my final secondary school exams approached, I felt completely overwhelmed, and lost my motivation to study. At one point I even considered not sitting my exams, almost following my father's footsteps. Now, looking back, it could have had dire consequences. Thankfully I was able to summon enough determination to sit my exams but, although I did well enough to get a place in university, I didn't get into medical school.

This engendered the first fork in my career journey. I could have taken a year out, sat my exams again and tried to make the sufficient score. Or I could move on, quieten the inner calling and follow the pressure to build a career that would be aspirational, solid and steady. I decided to move on and became an accountant.

Surprisingly, at the time, I didn't think much about this change of direction. Perhaps, deep down, I was ambivalent about medicine, or maybe I was just numb from the loss of my aspiration to become a doctor. Whatever the reason, I felt a desire to move on with my life, leave the small town behind, and free myself from the overwhelming expectations of my family. Accountancy felt like a respected profession, one that would be 'safe' and would fulfil everyone's hopes for me.

So, in 2002, instead of starting medicine, I started my commerce degree in Dublin. Reflecting twenty years later, I can see that there are many commonalities between medicine and accountancy. A curious analytical mind is needed. Emotional intelligence is important to being both a good leader and a good doctor. Ultimately much in both of these careers comes down to relationships. You build a relationship with your patient in order to understand their story, support them with their journey and help them heal themselves. Business is similar; it's only via the relationships you build that you succeed, gathering the information, and acquiring the right data for decision making.

However, as I progressed through my financial training, I still felt a yearning for my original calling. I found ways to keep medicine in my life, which included volunteering with the Red Cross, and satisfied my desire to help others. I attended a first aid course, progressed through my pre-hospital training, crewing ambulances and also advancing through the governance side of the organisation. I gained many skills and experiences in the ten years I was a Red Cross volunteer. There too I sought recognition.

By this point, I had already found an additional way to help my community: politics. My family has a proud political history. As a child, my great-great-grandfather's medals, awarded for his contribution to Irish independence, were framed over the mantelpiece in the sitting room at home. I became very active in student politics while at university and continued to pursue political work during my accountancy training. Aged 24, I ran for election as local councillor in my county, driving miles, knocking on doors, and visiting agricultural fairs to understand people's concerns and present my manifesto. Once election day came, however, I suffered a searing disappointment. This rejection stung. Looking back, I can see it also put me in touch with my falling short of medical school entry but I didn't yet have the maturity to see these setbacks as opportunities for growth. As before, moving on felt like the only way out and, as many Irish young people were doing at the time, I emigrated to the UK. My business degree and financial training at a high-profile firm had set me up for a good job in London.

I moved to the UK in 2009, in the middle of a financial crisis, transitioning from a professional services firm into industry, a path trodden by many. Working across a number of companies, I had the chance to understand different working environments. I have always been motived by challenge, be it in work tasks, or managing relationships; however, despite these roles generating sufficient challenge, I still felt unfulfilled, and I found myself wondering if I would rather be doing something else with my life and career. I am not sure that at the time I was fully aware of why, but I knew it just wasn't right for me. Reflecting on it now, I can see the need for recognition definitely played a part. I've always worked hard, but it wasn't always recognised. When it was acknowledged, I was happy, motivated and productive. When it wasn't, the opposite.

Parts of the job were great, however. I felt I was progressing in my career, and I saw how I could take on leadership roles in the future, acquiring a broad range of skills and planning out the next twenty years. There was a clear path. My next role was a sideways move, into the aviation industry, a sector I'd had a geeky interest in ever since I had been on my first plane journey. I hoped I had found a company where I could work for many years, a place to give me security and continuity. Whilst the initial role wasn't ideal, I hoped to use this as a springboard into something more senior.

I have come to realise that job security is very important to me. Part of this comes from my parents. For them, having a secure job was vital: get an education, the job would follow, and then you don't have to worry. A larger part comes from a lack of self-worth, a feeling of deep insecurity where I have a constant worry that things might be taken away from me. I also was brought up on a diet of Irish folk songs, documenting the Irish who came to the UK before me who ended up desolate, lonely and dying in poverty. Despite my education, and 'achievements' to date, I still worry that my life might go that way. Over time I have understood how this insecurity has shaped me and how it has foreshadowed other needs and aspirations I had for myself, and that would make me more intrinsically happy.

Despite my interest in the aviation industry, and the promise of security this role offered, I quickly drifted back into a feeling of frustration. The support and potential for career progression promised in the interview quickly evaporated and opportunities for growth turned out to be limited. I was working hard, regularly having to do 12-hour days, on top of a horrendous commute. When I approached the Head of Department for advice and a way forward, I found out I had been deliberately misled, and at least another two years of this faced me. Honesty is a value I feel strongly about, and I could not tolerate being deceived in this way. I had to leave. Moving on from this organisation, I took a role that was both interesting and more senior. However, during my interview, something didn't feel right about my boss, and I found the relationship difficult throughout the time we worked together. This manager was secretive; I had no idea of what exactly he was doing on a day-to-day basis and, although I had my suspicions, I never could really get to the bottom of it. In one way he let me get on with my job, as long as I delivered what he wanted, but I couldn't trust him. He wasn't supportive, and I felt he wasn't focused on me or his job. This again showed me the importance of integrity in our work, and indeed in all of our interactions with others. The working-class ethics of my upbringing, the importance of doing an honest day's work for an honest day's pay, shaped my work interactions and my expectations of others in the workplace.

I learned some important lessons from these experiences: firstly, to be aware that things aren't always how they are first presented. Secondly, trust your gut. If something doesn't feel right, challenge it, because you feel that way for a reason. Following your intuition can allow you to uncover the real facts of the case. In medicine, I have found my gut feeling invaluable in seeking out problems before they arise. Finally, my gut instinct led me to question do I really want to do this job? Working with others can be challenging but if I have purpose, if I am fulfilling a mission and a passion, I will thrive regardless of who I am working with.

These experiences also made me realise that I needed to rethink my career choices. By chance I was informed about the possibility of studying medicine as a mature student. This led me to wonder if the road that I left behind in my teenage years might not be foregone after all?

After much thought, I decided to return to university to study medicine. In some respects, it was a reckless decision. I had a good job, career prospects and once again the possibility of a role in politics.

It had been over ten years since my departure from Ireland, and the disappointing experience of running for local election in my early twenties. I was now able to reflect on my 'failures' with greater maturity and objectivity. The people who had been floating around the Irish political scene with me in the early 2000s were now MEPs, Members of Parliament and government ministers. Some of them had setbacks along the way, like I did, but kept going. As I matured through professional and personal experiences, I came to understand that failure, sometimes multiple failure, can eventually lead to success. Looking back, I can see my first foray into politics was also an attempt to fulfil my need for recognition. By the time I was elected as a local government councillor in the UK in 2014, my perspective had changed. It wasn't so much about me but more about the community I served. This perspective also now guides my approach in medicine. In medical training we were often told to look only at the individual in front of us. I think this misses a large part of the picture. The joy of general practice is an ability to understand the patient in the context of their family, their community and the society they live in. I have become more and more aware of the impact of life, in the form of work, housing, relationships, on the health and happiness of individuals. I find myself also becoming more vocal on these issues as a doctor. In medicine, the personal is political. Perhaps my medical and political lives will cross in the future. But for the moment I know my medical career requires exclusive focus.

People are often surprised when I mention I returned to university as a mature student. To many, going back to studying feels like an incredible challenge. To some extent, in becoming a doctor, I was once again choosing a difficult task in order to feel special, be recognised and praised. The need to achieve and work hard has been often at the front of my decision making. This provided me with the grit and motivation to apply for and get a place on a medical course. Looking back now, I often ask myself, have I done it for the right reason, or am I just trying to prove a point and please someone?

Back in August 2013, with an air of excitement and nervous anticipation, I took my place on the graduate medical programme. I arrived with the expectation that it would be a programme tailored for professionals, with the standards that one would expect, having worked for a professional services firm. I was one of only a handful who had professional experience; most had just completed an undergraduate degree and were fresh from university learning. There was no room for tailoring to specific needs or requirements, nothing to consider how I might learn best and how to bring my skills to the front. Instead, just an abridged curriculum and a target: pass the exams and complete the year. My grandmother was terminally ill at the time, and I wanted to spend time with her towards the end. Support was limited; I was told to consider if I could manage to balance all life events and the demands of the course. Following some conflicting and unhelpful advice, I sat the end of year exams when my mind wasn't in the right place and, unsurprisingly, I failed. I was then given an ultimatum about what would happen if I took the resits and failed again: I would leave the course.

I had to pause, reflect, and with the help of friends, family and my therapist, I deferred, having to deal with only the second real failure of my academic life. In the way that becoming an accountant provided me with experiences I wouldn't have gained if I had gone straight to medicine, this setback provided me with other opportunities to grow. I took the time to complete three years of therapy, which has provided me with the skills of reflection and a better understanding of myself, which I otherwise would not have acquired.

Despite this, as a doctor in training, I have often been disappointed by the difference between my expectations and my experience. As trainees, we are assigned supervisors, but this supervision is often limited, light touch and rarely in the form that I would wish. It has often left me feeling demotivated. However, on the occasions when I have experienced good practice, and received the right support, I have been so much better for it. I am particularly exercised by this because it impacts on some of the things I deeply care abou; good leadership, well-run services and a happy motived staff. I experienced this acutely during the first wave of the COVID-19 pandemic. We were all sinking under the increasing number of patients being admitted, on-call shifts were understaffed, and we were all worried about how things would progress. A number of colleagues and I approached the senior medical team to change rotas, recruit more staff, redeploy others and make our working environment safe and manageable. Eventually we got there, but the sense of learned helplessness from others was disappointing.

Why do I feel this way? Is it more about me than the organisation? Or a mixture of both? Do I get frustrated because I am a perfectionist, or is it because I see how poor leadership in organisations fails patients at the most vulnerable place? The interplay between my values and my personality, what I know about myself and how I experience organisations, continues to influence my day-to-day working life.

I have been thinking a lot over the last few months about the chasm between how an organisation is perceived from the outside and how it feels working within it. Only recently I was asked to speak about my experiences over the last year, working on the 'frontline' during the COVID-19 pandemic, as one of the NHS "heroes". In society at large, the NHS is spoken about with a great degree of reverence. As Nigel Lawson once said, 'The NHS is the closest thing the English have to a religion', which makes the experiences of working in it often difficult. Some of this cognitive dissonance comes from the public narrative and the experiences within the organisation. The public expect the NHS to provide high quality, up to date care; however, they don't seem to be willing to pay for it. The lack of funding, coupled with cuts to social care, has made it more and more difficult to provide the care the public expect, and the care that we, as doctors, want to provide. I often find that I am unable to provide the care I want, due to lack of resources, poor systems or excess demand. This remains deeply frustrating.

Resilience is one of the themes I have had to consider, particularly in recent times. I struggle with how this word is often a synonym for pull up your socks, put on a brave face and just deal with it. Resilience to me is more about creating a supportive environment where staff can withstand adversity and even thrive despite it. There is definitely a culture of lip service to resilience in the NHS. A cash-strapped, burned-out organisation finds it easier to tell individuals to find the resources within themselves, rather than invest in an enabling environment that fosters resilience. Of course, caring for others at the most challenging times of their lives and being in life and death situations can be daunting. All heath professionals need to cultivate a backbone, or inner strength, in order to strive in difficult situations. In the past, I would have perhaps run away from these kind of challenges. But now I know this is not the answer. Instead I wonder about how we can find happiness and a sense of self in the workplace, and what organisations and leaders need to do to foster this culture.

So, did I make a mistake in changing career as I did? I would be lying if I said that at times, especially over the last two years, I hadn't questioned my decision. In the face of doubt, I find myself reflecting on my underlying motivations in becoming a doctor, and often return to the death of my grandfather. His cardiac arrest was most likely due to a blockage of the vessels in his heart. Although we don't know the precise reasons, he most certainly had underlying risk factors. Had they been known and addressed, it might have prevented his death. Today, one of my first thoughts is how can medicine help long before injury strikes, and make tangible differences to people's lives. My training has taught me all about taking a history, performing an examination, making a diagnosis and creating a management plan. My feeling of helplessness as a child, following my grandfather's death, has strongly informed my belief in preventative medicine.

Over the last twenty years I have become more values-focused in my life, and this has also affected my decision making. This is true as much in medicine as it is in other parts of my life. Initially I was motivated by not wanting to feel helpless, and also by a need to be successful. Studying medicine was seen as something which "successful" people did, and that was important for me. Over time I have become more and more focused on only doing things that align with my values. These values are at times muddled, but essentially come down to being helpful, caring and wanting to do the best by people. Medicine at the best of times achieves these goals. This sense of value is one of the main things that keeps me going on the bad days, of which over the past two years there have been many. When I can help people, it gives me a wonderful sense of satisfaction. I have worked in really challenging areas of London and this has given me purpose to work with some incredibly vulnerable people.

All of this has allowed me to see medicine with a broader lens; the impact of thousands of decisions, some good, some bad, on me and others. In my journey I have learned a lot about myself and those around me. I have discovered the root of some of my original motivations, and how they have changed. I realise now that a lot of my decision-making has come from a need for recognition, and a desire for praise. I realise that I have placed a high value on hard work, and pleasing others but question if this is the right way to go forward. Through these experiences I have managed to identify what will be important for me to work on in the future.

Firstly, I have learnt the importance of building a resilience which recognises my own needs as well as the needs of others. Recently I realised that one of the things I needed to do for myself was to arrange some time off, to spend with my partner and to recharge. My view of resilience is no longer just about pushing on, it's a much broader understanding of working in a healthy and balanced way which sometimes contradicts the more conventional view of resilience which I discussed above. I am now beginning to understand that putting myself first allows me to serve my patients better in the long run.

Secondly, I am really aware of a need to find true meaning in my life, and that comes from a place inside me. I have spent the last twenty years trying to be extraordinary. I only recently understood it is ok to be ordinary. I have always been motivated by extrinsic factors, of which the seeking of and need for recognition was top of the list. I recognise now that this is a fragile foundation on which to build your career success and I need to look deeper to find true meaning. This has come from understanding myself better. If I'd had this self-knowledge twenty years ago, I might have made different decisions about my future.

Thirdly, I need to work on my own happiness. These last two years have shown us how fragile life is. Finding the things that give me joy and prioritising them is something I need to do more of and something I plan to work on in the coming years.

Finally, I recognise that central to all that is how I work with other people, how I understand and relate to their needs and how to grow into a leader who understands the motivations of others. I am still going through a period of self-discovery, which I intend to continue. In many ways this process of development never ends, as it is always necessary to grow. In many ways, my career journey is only at its beginning, but I hope the reflections and experiences I have gained so far will help me be a better leader in the future.

CHAPTER SIX

Thriving at Work

A RESPONSE TO GERARD FROM SUSIE

> She stood in the storm and when the wind did not blow her way, she adjusted her sails.
>
> Elizabeth Edwards

When you hear the word "resilience" what image do you conjure up? A soldier in battle fatigues? A climber ascending the summit of Everest? A refugee arriving in Europe after a long and hazardous journey? Or a man like Gerard who decides to step away from his comfortable existence in finance to start the long journey of training to be a doctor? It's easy to contrast this with your own experiences and feel as though you are falling short, believing that you need some sort of supreme mental toughness to survive and flourish at work. The nineteenth-century social reformer Henry Ward Beecher (i) declared, 'Hold yourself responsible for a higher standard than anybody else expects of you. Never excuse yourself. Never pity yourself. Be a hard master to yourself – and be lenient to everybody else.' This seems pretty daunting and a recipe for unhappiness and exhaustion.

When the going gets tough, the tough get going?

Resilience has often been used to refer to behaviours that I believe can actually diminish one's resilience, such as relentless persistence, not showing emotion and going it alone. Resilience then becomes a synonym for becoming superficially strong and tough. This can often lead to unhappiness and burnout at work. Steven tells us in chapter thirteen: 'In Moscow, with no personal life, living apart from my new wife, whom I had met just as I was leaving Hong Kong, I gave everything to my work – long hours and six-day weeks. I slipped into familiar old patterns. That was when my blood pressure blew up.' Much of the 'wisdom' on resilience has been counterproductive: not showing emotion to avoid vulnerability. We hear mantras such as 'going it alone shows strength', 'perseverance no matter what'. This may serve us well in the short term but might there be other more sustainable strategies we can employ?

The global pandemic was profoundly challenging and relentless for all of us. It placed huge demands on our psyches. Many of my clients were working from small bedrooms, isolated from their colleagues. Some had the challenge of balancing work and educating children from home. The digital age has placed increased demands on our time, socially, economically and intellectually. Working days are 1.7 to 2 times longer than ten years ago and social media has accelerated the pace and volume of the data that we process and use to inform our decisions. The notion that we will stay in one career or work for one employer has long gone and in its place is the pressure that is created to manage your own working life and build multiple work identities.

When you have arrived in a new role there is then the pressure to be successful, to be available 24/7 and to demonstrate that you are coping. In fact, not just coping, but positively thriving. The reality can be very different. My client, Alice, explains how her life began to unwind; 'The long hours, the travel, the pain and the helplessness took their toll. The breakdown of a long-term relationship, under-investment in friendships, a quarter-life crisis, crippling panic attacks. I burned out.'

Taking a more agile perspective

We know that resilience has been identified as a key component of mental and physical well-being, so is there a better way of exploring the concept and, if so, how can we better equip ourselves to cope with career challenges? What if we conceived of it as the ability to be flexible and adaptable? The ability to grow, adapt and perform through times of change and challenge? This could blend being prepared and responsive with cultivating an ability to learn and develop. It's then much more dynamic and can be developed in times of low stress, not just in the face of challenge.

REFLECT

→ **Support**
How proactively do I use my relationships?
Do the people in my life know what I need in terms of support?
Where might there be gaps in my social support?

→ **Confidence**
What kinds of goals do I set myself?
Do I push myself out of my comfort zone?
What meaningful goals can I set for yourself now?
How self-aware am I?
What might build my self-awareness to enable me to play to my strengths?

→ **Striving**
To what extent do I persevere?
Can I find multiple ways around obstacles?
Do I know what brings you meaning?

→ **Recovery**
Do I know what builds or depletes my energy?
Am I proactive in how I manage this?
How could I create habits to support behaviour change?

→ **Changing**
How much am I looking ahead and proactively adapting to the changing context?
How could I apply my learnings from my experience more intentionally?

Who can support you when faced with challenge or one those big tough life questions? The pandemic has helped us to understand how interconnected we are and how much we need to rely on each other for support. Many of us have, seeped into our psyches, the belief that we must face things on our own, that we must be independent and it's 'weak' to ask for help. Maybe it's the relationship 'dowry' we inherited from our parents or our wider community. Can we recognise when help is needed? Serena, who writes her story in chapter fifteen, found herself in an uncomfortable place in her early forties. She told me when I was working with her that 'I had a mid-life work crisis around the age of forty. This centred on being heard, being me and being free to express what I wanted to express, I wanted to break free from the commitment, vocation and emotional ties of being an actress.' Serena shared her thoughts with a close circle of friends and her mentor and began to think about how she might find a place where she could use her gifts and process the negative emotions that she was feeling. She wanted a 'more nourishing working life' and explains the process: 'I had my first experience of being listened to without interruption, and I learnt to offer that simple discipline to others in a group or coaching context.'

How can you offer support to others around you? Gerard understands how vital this is: 'Resilience is one of the themes I have had to consider, particularly in recent times. I struggle with how this word is often a synonym for: pull up your socks, put on a brave face and just deal with it. Resilience to me is more about creating a supportive environment where staff can withstand and even thrive despite adversity.'

Show yourself some loving kindness

Self-compassion is hard to do but very important if you are going to support yourself and work through those negative emotions. What does it mean? Self-compassion entails being warm and understanding toward ourselves when we suffer, fail, or feel inadequate, rather than ignoring our pain or flagellating ourselves with self-criticism. Self-compassionate people recognize that being imperfect, failing, and experiencing life-difficulties is inevitable, so they tend to be gentle with themselves when confronted with painful experiences rather than getting angry when life falls short of set ideals. Self-compassion involves recognising that suffering and personal inadequacy is part of the shared human experience – something that we all go through rather than being something that happens to "me" alone. At the same time, mindfulness requires that we don't get stuck right in our thoughts and feelings, so that we are caught up and swept away by negative reactivity.

Confidence is important too, the capacity to build belief in our ability to achieve goals. Take a look at my essay on being brave, chapter two. Gerard realises that a financial career is not making him happy and reflects that: 'I decided to return to university to study medicine. In some respects, it was a reckless decision. I had a good job, great career prospects and the possibility of a political career.' Experience had given Gerard the chance not only to understand his strengths and saboteurs but to be able to draw on these to make a decision about his future. He also had the courage to seek out this new challenge and leap into the unknown. He knew he was quitting a well-paid, secure job but didn't let this overwhelm him.

Striving towards a goal can be powerful. I like to think about striving as moving towards a goal that is meaningful to you and keeping on going with it, but maintaining some fluidity and flexibility so that the goal doesn't become too rigid. I worked with a client who created a spreadsheet detailing the month she would get married, have a baby, get promoted and start her own business; we can recognise this might be doomed. Set yourself goals but acknowledge that you may have to shift a little. Angela, in chapter one, leaves her role in communications and sets herself a goal to become a writer and finish her novel. She explains, 'What if I began to write, seriously write? What if I began to act as if – no matter how unlikely – I wanted that to be my career? What then? Suddenly, I had a goal. A far-off goal, a goal most people don't ever reach, but a goal nonetheless. I could begin to build a working life around this goal.' It's now two years later and she has had to maintain some freelance communications work and reconfigure some of her writing projects.

But she is still on track and has had her first novel accepted by an agent.

Reinvigorating enables you to be at your best and re-energise after setbacks. I like to use the four energies model developed by Steve Radcliffe in the early 2000s (ii). Take a look and consider how you are doing on the four dimensions below.

THE FOUR ENERGIES

PHYSICAL ENERGY
Our physical energy drives our everyday performance levels. It's about sleep, eating well and exercise. It's how we show up in the world, when we are interacting with others, our physical 'presence' that enables us to keep active, moving and replenished.

INTELLECTUAL ENERGY
Our intellectual energy is that which focuses on data, on ideas, on logic and rationality. It's our ability to debate, articulate and conceptualise. This energy enables us to innovate, organise and move forwards.

EMOTIONAL ENERGY
Our emotional energy is our ability to relate to others, to build rapport and to engage. It's about empathy, our desire to understand, to listen and to explore our feelings. This energy is essential in creating engagement, followership, partnership and establishing collaborative ways of working.

SPIRITUAL ENERGY
Our spiritual energy is our focus on our purpose, our vision for ourselves and the values that we bring to our work. Our spirit energy enables us to focus on our future possibilities.

Setbacks are normal and we all need to attend to different energies at different times. Sarah, in chapter seven, describes the toll that young children take on her intellectual and physical energy. After being made redundant, she took a break and found that her spiritual energy was rejuvenated: 'It's given me time to reflect on what is important to me in all aspects of my life: finding balance and enjoyment and the importance of not losing oneself.' Reinvigorating can also be about celebrating and reflecting. Cassie, in chapter nineteen, explains: 'Sometimes success at work is too closely linked to how I feel about myself. I've learned that I need to remind myself to stop and celebrate a success – instead of rushing on to the next, to see what can be done better next time.'

Resilience is also about being adaptable. How do we learn from past experiences to form new perspectives for the present? We must let go of any thinking that doesn't seem relevant to the current context and generate new opportunities to pursue. All the writers in this book have lived through big changes socially, economically and environmentally and have been brilliantly adaptable and responsive to change. They have also taken the time to deeply reflect on what they care about and how they can create their own definitions of success. They are applying their learning in an intentional way. Sean, in chapter three, is embarking on a new career with a different quality of mission as he describes: 'The reason I'm leaving the career I've loved is, ultimately, because the impact of even the most insightful powerpoint presentation can never measure up to the emotional realities and life experiences of people who exist outside of the corporate bubble.'

Resilience is ultimately about building the mindset and tools for longevity; the type of longevity that keeps you feeling that you are flourishing in your career, that you are seeking support from others and that you are creating a diversity of life experiences that you continuously learn from.

It's about being self-compassionate and allowing your feelings to exist in the first place, expressing those feelings, and working through them.

CHAPTER SEVEN

Navigating the Rush Hour

SARAH

Whilst having a biopsy my dad was asked about his profession. As chief chaperone and moral support that day, I started to reply proudly on his behalf that he worked in TV. Dad mustered the energy to add, 'It's better than working for a living.'

What Dad conveyed in his characteristically low-key way was that his career had been his passion. He loved it. He was the man that made airwaves reach your TV and appear on screen. Pure engineering wizardry and magic. Leaving school at 14 to help out financially at home, he began fixing TVs and worked his way steadily up to global sport and news broadcasting. Dad's achievements were talent driven, not ambition driven. He was a real expert with no desire to be the big boss.

He did, of course, step into leadership roles a number of times: he enthused people with his passion, rather than a game plan. This is something that as a leader myself I hold in mind. I also find myself, like Dad, not really wanting to stand out: I passionately want success and results, yet slightly shudder internally when I'm in the limelight.

This, I am realising now, could mean I am perhaps more of an introvert than I'd previously thought – and might also be a sign of low confidence. Either way, I have masqueraded to the contrary for some time and developed a set of coping tactics: being a good reflective listener, doing my reading and research, preparing ahead of time to know what I want to say or do, going over an approach or idea in my mind to test it out.

My mum, in contrast to Dad, is driven as well as ambitious. Talented and with a passion for early years education, mum sought out promotions, leadership positions and progression. She is tough and resilient. She has lived with MS for over forty-five years and graduated from university at 32 with two small children. She doesn't accept being told "no" lightly.

Growing up, I watched Mum work late nights and weekends while my dad worked long shifts but did not bring his work home. They both have extraordinary work ethics stemming from their working-class upbringing. This is something they have instilled in both me and my sister: they worked hard to give us chances they didn't have, and we don't want to let them down. It's fair to say that both of my parents are equally dedicated and conscientious. They have given me a foundation of commitment, a sense of duty and the need to always try your very best. The flipside is potentially negative: holding oneself to high standards or a sense of guilt if you feel you have let someone down or fallen short. These feelings can make you feel that you are often failing to hit the mark and over time that can eat away at you. It makes it hard to celebrate your own successes if you find it hard to recognise when you've done well.

I can reflect now that, however unintentionally, my career – and my approach — is more like Mum's. From the start of my communications career, I was promoted quickly and took on bigger projects and started managing other people early on. My natural creativity came to the fore and was recognised and my tenacity meant that I would put ideas forward and be heard. Combined with hard work and attention to detail, my managers and I could see I was getting results and that led to greater responsibility. I relished this and the trust that came with it. I felt like I was progressing and developing and loved the mix of skills needed, the people and the variety of work.

I began my career three years before the world skidded into the 2008 recession. After briefly flirting with the idea of journalism and a stint as a TV news runner, I started working in technology PR. I was one of the early(ish) millennials in a Gen X world. Rather than agile workplaces where you bring your whole self to the office, the attitude was one of 'don't bring your personal life to work' and 'keep your head down'.

I started out on the cusp of a new approach to work and feel lucky to have a dual perspective of working in cultures driven by Gen X leaders and tech-savvy millennials who crave interesting work. There are pros and cons to both. Mostly though I view this dual perspective as a positive, allowing me to more easily navigate the different currents running through teams and organisations. Interestingly, some of the most successful and harmonious teams I have recruited and led have had a good diversity of age.

On paper, I had hit my career running but felt there was also something holding me back: if I made a mistake or if something didn't quite land as intended, I ate myself up for days … weeks … months! That continues to be my Achilles heel today. Reflection is good, while spiralling into a debilitating and anxious gloom is not. There is a tension between my drive, my confidence and not wanting to stand out too much. I am more aware of this now and realise how much of a contradiction it is. I also think I have hidden this well for a long time.

While my wavering confidence doesn't restrict me, it does take its toll emotionally. With time and age I'd like to think I can handle it better. With successes under my belt, I can be more confident in my approach. When personal doubts creep in I try to reason with myself. Yet, I also know how words and actions of others can still shoot a dose of cortisol into my system: my physical and emotional reactions can be visceral, yet concealed.

The reason for concealing my emotions is perhaps because I have, for too long, seen it as a weakness. It also shows, I think, a great deal of control when hiding it, which is energy that could be applied in a more useful way. I know that it is high time I recognised the value of this sensitive approach, rather than seeing it – or feeling it – as a flaw: it is that same sensitivity which brings out empathy, understanding and kindness in my leadership style. These are positive traits that have often been highlighted by my managers and my teams.

Reflecting back a few years now, I remember how my employer nominated me for an industry '30 under 30' award: all I had to do was sign the final submission. The deadline happened to fall on a nightmare day, during which a government special advisor was yelling down the phone at me because their team hadn't kept them updated with plans for a (very senior) minister. I took it so personally, I felt like a fraud and wouldn't submit the entry. How could I fool myself and enter when clearly I was totally inept?

The problem had not been of my making – I knew then, and I know now. I was also in receipt of a commendation from my employer and statements of endorsement from industry leaders and the kind support of a journalist peer. Perhaps I had let them down by not submitting the entry. I was so busy feeling awful about the situation that I am not sure I properly considered how all those people who had helped me might have felt.

I know now that I really was a fool not to enter. But that feeling of being an imposter or falling short is a hard one to beat, for me. Where does that come from? I do set high standards and don't want to fall short. The root of the problem could be one that stopped me taking extra time in exams for my dyslexia: people would notice, I would stand out, and then what would they think of me? I know it is completely self-limiting: extra time and reducing the pressure on myself would have led to better exam results, options and opportunities.

There are definitely competing forces at play here: a desire and energy to lead, yet being a little afraid of standing out too much. I hope, in actuality, this makes me an empathetic and generous leader who ensures everyone has their moment to shine. I have always committed to spending valuable 1:1 time with my team members, worked hard to push them forward for opportunities, tried to understand what would we could do together that would help their next career move, and most importantly celebrate successes. I also underpin all of this with accountability so we could have honest conversations about what is working and what is not.

Fast forward over a decade into my career and I had my first baby. I'd been promoted to director a few months before, my team was in great shape and things were going well. Outside of work my husband had opened a restaurant to critical acclaim and our friends around us were having kids too. I had a glorious maternity leave: baby music, baby yoga, baby gym. I poured all my energy and headspace into this tiny and magical little being. After years of being a slave to email and being immediately available on the mobile, I loved the newfound baby bliss and the very different pace and focus.

I'd kept in touch with my team around times of appraisals, attended the senior leadership away days and was in contact with the wonderful woman covering my role. Even so, 'switching back on' properly for my return to work was a shock to the system. There was a pull of being a parent: the focus of my attention was no longer linear and my energy was depleted. Let's just say it's like going to work after a long-haul flight every day while pretending to be a perky air steward 24/7.

It also struck me that, while on maternity leave, I'd been overlooked for the chance to go for a promotion. On every practical level it made sense, because I wasn't there to do the job. But there was still something that stung. This was the moment that my pacey career began to stagnate – and the first time I felt like 'a woman in the workplace'.

I returned when morale in my team was at a low. They had been pretty neglected when it came to fighting their corner for pay rises and our budget had been cut. I was sad that what I'd built was no longer working smoothly. I also felt that colleagues were expecting me to be just as I was before the baby, but I didn't feel the same 'me' any more: my life had changed a lot in a short space of time, my energy levels were different, my brain felt different, my priorities felt different. People hit different life stages across their career: how can we be better prepare ourselves – and our workplace cultures – for such changes?

To perform well I needed to start rebuilding the team and delivering results. There were mountains to climb in the day and a baby to soothe at night. Arguably I could have looked to share some of the load, but like many working parents I just assumed I needed to get on with it and make it work.

We knew we wanted a second child and moving jobs to chase a promotion didn't feel like the right move for our family. Nonetheless I was conscious of wanting my next challenge. With this feeling of stagnation starting to take hold, I relished the opportunity to take on voluntary roles outside of work, in education and the arts, which have always been passions of mine.

For one of the roles, I was heavily pregnant when I arrived for the interview in the pouring rain, bedraggled and conscious that my yellow suede shoes might have been a bad choice. If I'd felt overlooked or the tiniest bit aggrieved about the lack of workplace promotion, my faith was restored when the board offered me a role – a board that had significant experience and which, to their credit, wanted to bring in young blood. It was a real honour to be offered the position: I felt like a grown-up with experience and opinions that were fully recognised and valued.

On my second maternity leave, I paid less attention to what was happening at work because I knew that changes would happen with or without my attention. I loved having my voluntary roles to keep my head in the game. My first board meeting after my second baby was born was when he was just seven weeks old. My husband sweetly chaperoned me there. I fed the baby in the park in the 2018 heatwave, went to the meeting, popped out to feed in the break, and went back.

A few months later there was an away day and the South East was covered in snow. I left the baby for the first time overnight and headed off with a breast pump. I was hoping that I could string a sentence together, offer some useful contributions and take some unnoticed 'comfort breaks'. I did what I often do when feeling a little out of my depth: I went all in. I spoke to everyone, tried to roll out simple questions (often the best ones) and look at things from different perspectives. I tried to find commonalities with my new peers, wore a huge smile (doesn't help with gravitas though) and hoped for the best.

There is definitely an element of people pleasing in my approach – especially when my sensitivity takes the lead and my confidence is buried somewhere deeper inside. I do need to keep this in check though as I am also tenacious and will push for an outcome I believe in. People can find that a bit inconsistent, confusing and, possibly, infuriating at times. In short, being gentle shouldn't be confused with being a walkover.

Having a baby does something to your brain. To me, it feels a bit like someone has shaken out a good deal of your vocabulary, leaving me grasping for words that once came freely. There are lots of reasons for this: neurological, hormonal, lack of sleep and simply juggling a lot more in your head (and with your arms) at any given moment than ever before. No wonder so many women have a dip in confidence after having children as there is so much competing for your headspace; you want to do everything well and worry that you're not doing any of it well at all.

After maternity leave round two, I returned to the same organisation for the second time, knowing that it was really time for me to move on. I needed to do six months back in the role and from there my plan was to make a move just as soon as I'd finished some high-profile projects. And then the COVID-19 pandemic hit. Any plans to change jobs would have to wait again.

I spoke to Susie a couple of weeks into lockdown one. 'How are you, Sarah?' she asked. I had absolutely no idea how to answer that question. Underfoot I had an eighteen-month-old that my four-year-old regularly tried to cuff around the ankles with plastic handcuffs while I attempted a day of back-to-back Zoom calls. Susie asked how my team were. She asked how, as a leader, I had or could respond to support the team; what would be useful? How could we be empathetic with one another and more than that, compassionate? What team development work could I do in this time and how could we use the time to experiment?

I was so grateful for that call: all of the questions were clues about moving forward beyond the shock of what was happening around us.

The first step was to "fess up" about the realities of being a working parent in lockdown: yes, my team knew I had two young children under foot, but no, they did not know what that meant. Fortunately, my female boss and mum-of-three was acutely aware of what juggling a family and job was like in that new world of WFH. Slowly, and with the aid of a global pandemic, I think I am coming to terms with the idea that superwoman is a fictional character and not a realistic expectation of working and being a parent in the twenty-first century.

There is a lot I did professionally during that first and second lockdown that I was proud of both personally and with the team. But it was against a challenging backdrop. For me, leadership is a lot about confidence and trust: that others have confidence and trust in you and that you have it in those around you. When doubts creep in, the culture of the team is disrupted. I started to feel this in my team for the first time and it did not feel good or healthy.

My confidence in my own leadership wobbled after some unpleasant and vexatious allegations were made against me. The organisation was slow to act and it was a painful, protracted and emotionally draining experience. With home and work blurred due to lockdown, the impact was felt by the children and my husband alike. With no physical or mental place to go for escape, I was penned into a horrible work experience 24/7 for months, unable to put in a divide between work and home and unable to take control of the situation myself. I felt powerless; for me, the psychological contract made with my workplace was now in question.

I learnt a lot about resilience in that period. I carried on, was professional, supported the team, worked to develop the team where I could and delivered everything expected of me (and hopefully more). But I did feel terribly let down and, most of all, I felt sad that the stress severely impacted family life. I struggled to be the mum I wanted to be in that period and that was heartbreaking. My energy was through the floor, I was snappy, I worked long hours, I was emotionally exhausted and every grown-up conversation was dominated by work.

That shouldn't be the experience of work: to feel constantly stressed, to feel a situation is unjust and you are powerless and that your whole life is affected. This experience will stick with me. I have no doubt it will shape what I am prepared to take on and not to take on in the future. It's also made me question a part of my working life I have always loved: building, managing and leading a team.

Unusually, I was not hiding my new state of mind well. A peer asked me where my ambition was. It knocked me sideways. Had it really gone? And if so, where? And why? Either way, I sure as hell wanted it back. My confidence was at rock bottom and my sensitivity was turned to max.

This question turned out to be an important one at the right time. It forced me to recognise that things were out of whack. The tension I'd always had between drive and confidence had given way to doubt and anxiety.

I was feeling somewhat drained. Needing change, I jumped at the opportunity for voluntary redundancy when the window opened. I'd long known I'd outgrown my role and wanted to move on. The timing coincided with my parents needing a lot of my time and support: my dad had just been diagnosed with a progressive and advanced cancer and my mum had broken her back.

Managing my father's care brought out my natural tenacity, compassion and need for answers and solutions. It has been my most challenging role yet: the desire to "fix it" and reach a neat goal is futile in the face of metastatic melanoma. Yet, I found that all of my professional skills have been needed: getting my head around complex issues, diplomacy, plate spinning, unafraid to phone, email, track down or chase people. I wasn't able to make Dad well again, but I could get stuff moving and get stuff done to help him.

Alongside the physical care, I cracked through obscene amounts of medical and domestic admin – again something that my career has prepared me well for. His misdiagnosis is now being investigated as a serious Incident by the Trust. Appointments and surgeries were moved forward. His desire to be home and not at a hospice was met. These were not small or insignificant to him – or to the rest of the family. There is nothing I could have been doing in a job that would have been so meaningful.

Stepping off the hamster wheel to be there for Dad was a privilege afforded by incredibly well-timed voluntary redundancy. Aside from the extra time with my dad, it's given me the opportunity to reflect on what is important to me in all aspects of my life: finding balance and enjoyment and the importance of not losing oneself.

For the next six to twelve months my goal is to build up a small client base of my own. In some ways this is going back to my communications agency roots – managing multiple projects and not being embedded in an organisation. It is also very much about honing in on my core professional skills, stripping back the management layers that come with being an employee and managing a function and team.

So far, so good. For a start, I have far greater control over my time, and without back-to-back meetings I can get my head down – it is such a luxury and in stark contrast to a day of meetings with a to do list that is double the length it was in the morning. It also means I can better manage my voluntary commitments too, building in time to deliver on the things I said I would, rather than squeezing them into the side lines and evenings.

Without a salary to fall back on, I have to keep moving and finding new projects – it is keeping me on my toes and, at the moment, that is energising. A little daunting but motivating to say the least.

But more than that, there is a really good sense of achievement in the projects I am creating and delivering, and I am receiving such positive feedback about my work and style it's been a real boost to my confidence already. And not just professionally either. One friend recently asked what I am up to at the moment: they felt I was more relaxed, more present and happier and they wanted 'whatever I was on'. A new contact described me as vivacious. It's been such a lift after quite a long time feeling less than vivacious, present and relaxed.

What I am realising is what I have to offer and to understand better my core professional skills and the many different aspects of my leadership skills — high ethical standards, diligence, diplomacy, loyalty and a firm belief in the value of collaborative working – that I need to pull on daily.

This move has also forced me to step forward as, when all is said and done, it is just me: my ideas, my work and down to me to deliver what I said I could. In many ways this is my most exposed, forward-facing role yet.

CHAPTER EIGHT

Work? Life? The Quest for Balance

A RESPONSE TO SARAH FROM SUSIE

> No, they didn't have any money, the sea was dangerous and men were lost, but it was a satisfying life in a way people today do not understand. There was a joinery of lives all worked together, smooth in places, or lumpy, but joined. The work and the living you did was the same things, not separated out like today.
>
> Annie Proulx *The Shipping News*

I didn't really understand what the phrase 'work-life balance' meant until I reached my thirties. At university I was rather unconsciously immersed in feeding my curiosity when studying psychology or indulging in less "worthy" pleasures and experimentation outside the library and the lecture hall. When I started work, I expected to work assiduously and this felt fun and pretty exhilarating. I had time at weekends and evening to see friends, travel and generally live with abandon. I don't think the late 1980s and early 90s were a time of great reflection on the meaning of the capitalist work ethic or the purpose and value of our careers, certainly not for me, anyway.

So much has changed for me since those hedonistic and somewhat naïve years. I have become a more reflective individual. Generations after me have demanded more from their working lives and the pandemic has caused many of us to press pause. I have found work that has felt truly meaningful and have wanted to immerse myself in developing a business, in learning and creating. This has meant, at times, that work has taken up a significant portion of my life. I find myself talking about work even more, but not quite sure what part it should play in my life. It was way back in 1843 when Thomas Carlyle (i) declared: 'A man perfects himself by working.' It seems that we are still very busy pursuing that goal. Technology has made it easy to be always "on the job". We are still exploring what place work has when perhaps other areas of life such as religious practice, tight community or extended family are no longer significant parts of day-to-day life. A job outside the home is often high status and domestic duties and childcare at home, because it isn't paid, is sadly traditionally less valued.

If you are reading this as an employer or as a manager, you will know that there is a real tension between providing good work-life balance and the reality of economic uncertainty. The quest for productivity of all kinds brings anxiety and insecurity into our workplaces. Post-pandemic, many of us have become used to more freedom in how we structure our working lives. A study by Aviva (ii) discovered that following the pandemic, we now rate work-life balance as more important than salary: 'More workers said they were attracted to their current role for the work-life balance (41%) than the salary (36%). This is a switch in rankings compared to 2019, before the pandemic.'

Life gets busy

Actually, my first personal provocation came when I became a parent. Soon after my first child it dawned on me that I would have to think about what I really wanted and how I was to juggle roles and multiple identities. Sarah, in her writing, explores the impact of this shift: 'There was a pull of being a parent; the focus of my attention was no longer linear and my energy was depleted.' She continues explaining the impact of motherhood with dark humour: 'It's like going to work after a long-haul flight every day while pretending to be a perky air steward 24/7.' Many of my male clients are, of course, exploring the impact of parenthood too, but it does seem to be women that articulate this more powerfully. Perhaps because the impact on women is often more profound and the burden of the care still is predominantly female.

The search for a balanced life is a hotly debated topic for everyone at all stages of our working lives. It can feel incredibly personal that we can't combine work and home life effectively, but I do wonder if twenty-first century notions of perfect parenting and the competitive nature of organisational life conspires against us in resolving these experienced tensions.

But the concept of finding work-life balance feels problematic because it implies that life only really happens when work stops. A depressing way to think about what constitutes the majority of our day. As you read the stories in this book, you will see the quest for fulfilment and the sheer joy when this is achieved at work. Reflecting on what you value is a challenging and an ever-changing process; take a look at chapter four on meaning and purpose to find out more. This reflection really helps in deciding how you want to spend your time. It will support you in deciding how to navigate the hours that you have available. If you decide that something is worth succeeding at, it helps you to understand why you are spending time working away at it.

Ami, in chapter nine, talks about a redefinition of her values in early mid-life. Again, after becoming a parent, she notes: 'Becoming a mother made me re-evaluate the time and energy I was investing in my career and accept that I wanted and needed balance. The things that really matter to me are quite basic: self-acceptance, family, friends, secure and content children who grow up to value and recognise their place in the world.' Ami has understood what flourishing looks like in her personal life. This personal life isn't about doing what others tell you to do, so why should work be? Ami understands these values are deeply intrinsic to her sense of meaning in life. Knowing this can get her through the tough times, perhaps attending to screaming toddlers, nursing sick children or sleepless nights. But often you also have to commit to and be good at your career so you can support yourself, and perhaps your family, financially. Work plays such a big part in our lives and the pressures to earn enough in the face of a soaring energy crisis, housing costs and just basically living mean that the quest for balance can feel pretty difficult.

Sacrifice or passion?

We often need to dedicate a huge amount of time and effort to doing something really well. Let's go back to Sarah's story. Sarah was a new parent, loving this time but recognising that she needed something else in her life. She had been treading water in her role since returning from maternity leave: 'I was conscious of wanting my next challenge. With this feeling of stagnation starting to take hold, I relished the opportunity to take on voluntary roles outside of work, in education and the arts which have always been passions of mine.' Sarah was aware that her life was a tough juggling act but despite this, she strove to include what she intrinsically valued in her life.

You might expect work to feel exhausting and maybe make you even a little miserable. Some of us expect work to be hard graft. How can you find the joy? Because the irony is that it's when you are feeling that sense of passion and excitement, as Sarah did, then that's the time that you can be truly successful in what you do. Can you shift your own mindset?

EXERCISE: Finding Balance

Have a go at the following questions when deciding how to spend your time:

→ What matters to me most here?
→ In which case what do I really want to make happen?
→ What bigger motivation or value of mine does this speak to?
→ How does doing this support something that really matters to me?

What does it take to free yourself from unhealthy ways of working and find a more sustainable and happy work-life balance? For many of us it can be really easy to lose our sense of proportion and begin to work very long hours. This can be driven by organisational expectations, fear of failure, presentism or a sense of duty. As many of us are working from home some of our week, we can easily feel "on" all the time and setting boundaries becomes so important.

Have a read of what my client, John, experienced recently: 'Working remotely was a very different prospect. I was lonely and communication/relationship building with clients and team members was challenging over Zoom. I felt very disconnected from the work and quickly became overwhelmed and unable to cope when I was appointed to manage an enormous project with a very demanding client on my own. This client called me all hours of the day and night and was a pretty erratic character. I also initially attempted to work four days a week (for 80% pay) but found myself working 60+ hours a week and hating it.'

Making changes

Does this resonate with you? In order for you to thrive, you have to set some boundaries, otherwise your capacity to be cognitively, emotionally and physically resilient will diminish. Try unruffled communication of your boundaries to others; this can be powerful because we treat ambiguity and uncertainty as a threat. When you are exhausted,you can get stuck on task and lose sight of the objective. I'm sure you really care about your work, but many of my clients care too much. They get involved in everything and become available at all hours to chat through any issues. They hold on to tasks that might easily be delegated elsewhere. How can you let go and therefore open up other parts of your life? What might you be assuming? How can you define your role to give yourself more space?

EXERCISE: Take a step back

Ask yourself, be specific: what is currently making me feel dissatisfied or unbalanced? How is that impacting my working life? My performance and the relationships that I have? How is this affecting my personal life? What is taking priority? What am I losing out on? Make some notes or find somebody to share your thinking with.

How can you recognise your emotional reaction to the situation? Awareness of and reflection on your emotional state is really useful and will help you make the changes that you want to. Remember how John felt when working so hard during Covid. Acknowledging these feelings allowed him to step back from them and see that he had some choice about how he worked; this wasn't his pre-ordained fate. It so easy to have a very emotional reaction to what we perceive as a stressful situation. Are you actually exhausted or frustrated? Or disengaged? What is the feeling signalling to you? I often work with clients where they have become emotionally stuck. The experienced emotion then results in a behaviour which might be problematic and become sabotaging. What was the root cause of fear of failure for my ferociously hardworking but burnt-out client? How does this impact him and others? How can he pay attention to other behaviours that might be being underused?

EXERCISE: Where do my priorities lie?

Ask yourself: what am I willing to sacrifice and for how long? Why?

Do I have any regrets? Might I have any in the future?

What specifically might I change in my job?

What would I like to spend time on that I am not doing right now?

The writers in this book and in my wider client practice have multiple and varied life/work challenges. Each individual makes different decisions when designing their version of the well-lived life. We have read about raising a child single-handed, working across the globe, changing career mid-life, leaving a secure role to become a writer or taking a year off to learn about social enterprise. These writers are lucky enough to be able to have choice and a large dose of self-determinism. They do this against the backdrop of society today, including rapid technological advances, the continued thrust for economic growth, post-pandemic and the climate crisis. Many of the writers are part of an organisational culture which can enable or create barriers to a balanced life. But we also can take individual responsibility to manage our behaviours.

How can you understand and manage these behaviours so that you can find healthy equilibrium in your own life?

CHAPTER NINE

The Examined Life

AMI

Following twelve years of struggling to find my place in the legal profession, eight years of intermittent therapy, six career coaching sessions, five years of motherhood and a few honest chats with good friends, I realised that I was in the wrong job and had got there for the wrong reasons.

Deciding to leave the profession that I worked so hard to get into has finally allowed me to show up as myself. Only now am I starting to discard some deep-rooted yet raw and present feelings of not belonging and this constant disappointment with my career.

During my early thirties I felt like I was spiralling. The same career frustrations were circling their way back into my life again. My counsellor reassured me that the spiral I spoke of was in fact a helix that I was climbing and I was making progress with every step. He pointed out that every time I encountered a difficult situation in the workplace, I was dealing with it in a better way than I previously had. But, despite making progress, I never felt content. I often attributed the discontent to not having the recognition or salary that I deserved. I also became a mother for the first time and this changed things in ways I did not expect. Raising my child threw me into a reflection of my own childhood that was both uncomfortable and revelatory. The journey has taught me to recognise and respect my own needs, not just the needs of those around me.

What strikes me about my career struggles to date is that they are intertwined with my wider struggle towards self-acceptance. My disappointments in the workplace included not qualifying as a barrister and pursuing a less prestigious route into the legal profession. Once qualified, I had to fight for equal treatment to my peers. Learning to balance the working mother tightrope after returning from maternity leave often left me feeling insecure. All these things were compounded by the complexity of office politics, perhaps the most difficult aspect of working life for me and often the source of much upset. Through the work I have done with Susie and my own reflections, I now recognise that I have control and authority over my career. I now feel in a position to use what I have learnt to realise the person that I truly am.

I grew up within and between two cultures. I was born and bred in leafy middle-class southwest London in the 1980s. This was a little more than ten years after my parents and their families, originally of Indian heritage, were displaced from their respective homes in East Africa. The richness of my cultural heritage had a positive influence in my life when it was not being belittled by ignorant or racist comments at school.

Many contradictions fed into my life and this contributed to me learning to adapt to whatever situation or group I found myself in. I learnt to appreciate our small two-bedroom flat above our grocery shop. I knew its size did not represent the cultural affluence I was born into. By the time I was seven, I had travelled to Kenya and India, and already felt more worldly than some of my privileged schoolmates. We had a big family, with hundreds of people who were a constant part of our life – there was no time to feel lonely as an only child. Our family was well-respected and prosperous within the Gujarati community and yet we always felt on the edge if not just outside white middle-class England. All my parents' friends were not only Gujarati but also from the same caste. Yet, as the only ethnic minority in my friendship groups, I always found a way to blend in. Despite being different, I found ways to muddle through the complexities of childhood and adolescence.

My parents had high expectations of me, perhaps linked to how hard they had worked to pay for my private education. When I got 96% in a Latin exam, my dad's first question: 'What happened to the other 4%?' I was rarely praised for my achievements and any recognition was always understated. 'They're only GCSEs,' was my dad's response when I got a flurry of A*s and As. I almost did not believe my friends who would tell me they got paid for doing house chores and felt envious at how they were celebrated for their successes.

There was a stark difference between what was culturally acceptable and expected by my family and what was normal practice in western society. Although my mum always worked, she was also the housewife and did all the cooking, cleaning and childcare. I recall the first time being at a schoolfriend's house and being quite shocked that her dad was making us dinner, having only ever seen my dad in the kitchen to eat.

Being an Indian female brought an added layer of pressure. There was so much I was not allowed to do because it would have been frowned upon. Socialising with boys was a no-no and having a boyfriend was not even worth contemplating. Smoking, drinking, and taking drugs were all taboo and considered shameful behaviour, especially for a girl. And whilst I did not actually follow these unwritten rules, I did have to keep the two sides of me quite separate so that I could engage with "normal" life on both sides.

Having found a way to lie to my parents quite comfortably, I was quite unaware of the lack of independence and agency in many of the choices I made. The expectations I faced contributed to me never feeling like I was good enough and in turn, I became a perfectionist; a defensive trait to shield myself from criticism.

Growing up, I had no idea that my family life and history would have such a significant impact on my education. I mostly did well at school although in the early years the teachers had concerns about my English. A teacher even went to see my parents at their shop and told them to stop speaking to me in their native tongue, Gujarati, as it was affecting my progress. (I now wonder whether those kids whose parents spoke Spanish, French or German at home had the same teacher visit.) In the subjects where I was doing well (everything except English and Art), my parents were frequently told that I was 'too chatty'. So, even when academically everything was going well there were always 'areas for development'.

This heightened my immigrant parents' ambitions and expectations around my education. Shaped by both their gratitude to this country for giving them a second chance and their innate belief in the importance of education, they had sent me to top private schools. However, they took a very narrow approach to my education; one which only had room for Maths, English and Science. The Arts and Humanities were largely considered irrelevant, not just by them but also the wider community we were a part of. The "wider community" (a sprawling network of extended family and friends) could not help but pry when decisions were being made about my education. It was entirely normal for my GSCE and A level choices and results to be openly discussed by others, while I would sit there, at times a mere spectator of my future. 'Languages? What will she do with Languages?' 'With those GSCE grades, I can get her in to any top dental school.' 'She could do Medicine if she wanted to.' Some of these comments were facetious while others were obviously well-meaning. I was however unaware of the weight of these words on how my future panned out.

When I eventually chose Spanish, History and English at A level, I thought that I was going against the grain and claiming my identity. I cannot recall my parents' reaction to this choice, but I do remember feeling like I had finally been able to direct my own future. I now understand that these choices were made as an act of rebellion rather than in pursuit of happiness.

Knowing that I was different from my schoolfriends gave me a ready-made identity in many ways. I didn't need to distinguish myself – my skin colour did that for me. Assumptions were often made about my family, our religious practice, even our diet. I managed to arouse interest without trying, and having to constantly battle with stereotypes and clichés meant that I was never a wallflower. This, coupled with my people pleasing tendencies, meant that I either played up to what was expected of me, or I completely defied it. I now recognise this as a tendency to act instinctively – another habit which I have carried into working life.

During university and immediately afterwards, I actually had very little clarity about my career path. Having studied Spanish, I initially considered teaching Modern Foreign Languages although it is difficult now to justify why or how I reached that decision beyond orchestrating an independent insurgence against the army of doctor and dentist cousins around me. As a slightly conceited twenty-something-year-old, I was quite convinced of my wisdom and ability to make a success of teaching despite having no pre-existing commitment to the profession. I was also influenced by narratives around studying languages at degree level, which were that career choices were limited to translation or teaching. The latter was more appealing to my sensibilities. I could see myself standing at the front of a classroom, telling a bunch of kids what to do while grasping a mug of tea and feeling important. After all, I was never one to shy away from being the centre of attention or doing all the talking. The truth is I do not remember writing my PGCE application to the Institute of Education, which perhaps conveys how little thought I put into it.

I do, however, remember the moment I found out that I had been rejected from there but was accepted at St Martins (a very respectable but less prestigious PGCE provider). I was volunteering as an English teacher in a small town called Urubamba in Peru and felt an enormous sense of relief that I had a reason not to pursue teaching anymore. A mixture of a smug sense of 'well if the best place does not want me, it's not for me', and relief that perhaps this was my opportunity to pick something that would win the approval of my family. And one phone call to my parents later, who were on holiday in India at the time, it was decided that I would do the Post Graduate Diploma in Law (GDL) and convert to become a lawyer.

To give this decision some more context, towards the end of my third year of university, whilst on my Erasmus year in Spain, I learnt that my long-term boyfriend, who was pretty much living with me, had been cheating on me. It was one of the most painful experiences of my life – he was my first love, the first and deepest wound and it took me the entirety of my twenties to recover. The heartbreak pushed me to reintegrate into my family, the wider community I have mentioned and further embrace my cultural heritage. The breakup is a large part of why I chose family approval over finding and pursuing my own needs. I was alone and I needed to feel part of something again. My family was there for me, silently relieved I was no longer dating a white man. Over the five years we were together, I had learnt to develop a version of me that suited him. It worked when we lived in different cities but once living together, I found it suffocating always subjugating elements of who I really was. The breakup felt inevitable but it also broke me. So, when I chose law, I was trying to fix myself by making my family happy and proud.

I can of course present a more erudite and persuasive explanation for how and why I chose that career path when needed. The raw truth however is that the decision was made instinctively in response to rejection. Law seemed like a natural fallback – a respectable profession and something to challenge me intellectually. I thought law would allow my parents to feel as though all their sacrifices to fund my education had been worthwhile.

By now I was also getting mixed messages from them, as they were now thinking about when I would get married. The pressure to succeed professionally was always somewhat contradicted by the expectation that I would also be a good Indian wife to someone one day. The tension between achieving career success and getting married has caused much anguish to many young Indian women for generations. Choosing to study law also gave me an excuse to avoid thinking about getting married and settling down for a while longer.

The two years studying the GDL and the Bar Vocational Course went relatively smoothly. I was not intimidated by a new and very extensive subject, and I did not once question whether it was the right career path. I had made the decision blindly but was genuinely absorbed by some of what I was learning.

The first time I felt truly ignited at law school was when a former death penalty exoneree called Nick Yarris came to speak about his experiences on death row and his subsequent release. I was very much provoked by the miscarriage of justice that he had experienced – twenty-two years in prison for a crime he did not commit. Twenty-two years fighting to clear his name through DNA evidence. During the same number of years that I had simply lived my life, Nick Yarris had fought to save his. I suddenly felt like the law carried a sense of purpose beyond the insipid features of a contract or a tenancy agreement. The law was also a vessel through which innocent people wrongly convicted of committing a crime could be vindicated. And in that moment, I realised that I could potentially have a meaningful career and contribute to making a real difference for people. This felt empowering and motivating.

As soon as I completed the Bar Vocational Course, I applied to undertake an internship with Amicus, a UK-based anti-death penalty charity. I spent three months in Mississippi at the Office of Capital Post Conviction Counsel working alongside some very inspiring attorneys who had dedicated their careers to representing convicted murderers and seeking a sentence of life without parole in place of the death penalty. What united all of us who worked there was that we strongly believed that no one deserved to die because of their actions. What divided those who still do that work and those of us who don't is harder to define. Towards the end of my time there, I had already become disillusioned with the lack of progress and the lack of visible results, despite the grind and emotional agony of the job. It was hard not to become emotionally attached to the clients, it was hard not to feel frustrated with colleagues who had learnt over the years to become less invested, and it was hard to feel like a failure in what is an ongoing, almost endless and historic struggle to end the death penalty. It is no surprise that I came back to the UK despondent and depressed.

Following my three-month stint in the US and notwithstanding the frustrations I encountered there, I entered private practice back in London with naïve expectations. I convinced myself that I wanted to be a criminal barrister and I came pretty close a couple of times, securing numerous second-round pupillage interviews over the years and a reserve place in one chambers, only to be pipped to the post by someone 'younger yet displaying equal ability' to my own. However, following a second-round interview at another set of chambers, I was only told that I was 'not a star'. It was hard to move forward from that kind of feedback. The pupillage interview process was chipping away at my confidence. I desperately tried to find professional support to help me get through the pupillage interview process but struggled to find someone willing to offer their time. I took it personally when people said they could not help me, and I found the additional layer of rejection more upsetting than motivating. For years I blamed myself for not making it as a barrister, punishing myself for "bad decisions" I had made in the early stages of my career that seemed to have a lasting impact.

Through the work I have done to reflect on my career, I have also considered and consolidated the experiences I gained during my education. I can now piece together how my childhood impacted on my career, particularly in how I chose to please others in an attempt to please myself, and acted instinctively in response to adversity. I now recognise that these decisions were often the reaction of my inner child, at times struggling to grasp the independence and agency right in front of me, and at times, protecting me from an actual bad decision.

By the time I was in my mid-twenties and working in the City, I had grown into a professional people-pleaser. This is a trait I have unwittingly carried into almost every workplace and it has held me back in ways I have only recently recognised and understood. Reflecting on this behaviour and its impact on me (and how others respond to me) has been transformative in every aspect of my life. Relying on making others happy in order to secure my own happiness was becoming a toxic trait for me. In starting to put my own needs first, I am in the process of identifying and evaluating what it is that I genuinely want from my career. Confronting memories from my childhood and education has been a critical part of doing this. I am still inclined to please others but now, with a stronger awareness of my habits, I try and do it more consciously and assertively.

Most of my twenties were spent in an extended state of teenage angst and, often, I felt like I was the only one still in this place. Most of my friends appeared to have both physically and emotionally detached from their parents. One of the complexities of the immigrant experience is a surplus of familial support which often manifests itself in expectation. I was still living at home and felt like I had to get my career right, in part because of my parents' financial investment in my education, and in part so that I could move out of home like my friends had.

Much of my energy seemed to be spent trying to find harmony and synergy between two opposing cultures. On the one hand, a young westernised woman working in London in the legal industry, seeking to make a mark and earn a seat at the proverbial table. On the other, an Indian woman with strong family values and an attachment to a vibrant cultural heritage, who really should be thinking about getting married. There were times I felt like I would have to pick one over the other because I simply could not see a way to comfortably be all of me.

In the workplace, this often resulted in my presenting a toned-down version of myself, not just from my Indianness but also from the core me. I adopted a work persona – one that I do not identify with now but can only be described as a very serious and perhaps lacklustre version of myself. I am not sure why I did this; it was not a conscious decision. On reflection, creating another version of me was a coping mechanism that I had developed to "fit in". It stood out most starkly when my supervisor made a leaving speech for me before I went on maternity leave towards the end of 2015. She described me as someone with a series of goals that I was seeking to tick off (qualifying, getting married and having kids), and that had successively been achieved through sheer drive and determination. I did not identify with anything she said about me, and I do not say that to be self-effacing. I genuinely did not (and still do not) relate to her description of me. My life had felt so much more confusing and chaotic than a series of goals to tick off.

Her speech was about "work Ami". It has taken me until now to realise what a wake-up call that moment could have been for me, had I not been distracted by impending motherhood. I suppose, in many ways, my reaction was a sort of *what the hell am I doing here, these people don't even know me?* moment and the beginning of my starting to question whether I really wanted that career for myself.

Perhaps one of the reasons I changed for work was because I always struggled with office politics; in particular, forming meaningful relationships with colleagues. With a tendency to take people and situations at face value, I struggled to grasp the subtext of certain decisions made in the workplace. In the early days of working, I foolishly believed that our primary responsibility was to provide the best possible service to our clients. I too readily wanted my colleagues to be my friends and believed that we would work together to act in the best interests of our clients. The reality, however, when working in private practice, was that our job as "fee earners" was to earn money for those at the top. Despite that collective label, it took me a while to fully appreciate that I was there to bring in revenue over and above anything else. As I gradually started to realise this, I became aware that I was easily replaceable. I struggled to find a sense of worth in being a fee earner by advising wealthy businessmen to fill the pockets of other wealthy businessmen. I knew that it was not sustainable for me long-term. However, I was also armed with my people-pleasing tendencies and my natural competence for the job. As a result, I always managed to achieve what was expected of me and a bit more, and often felt wanted and needed enough to stay rather than leave.

Through the process of reflecting and understanding the choices I have made to date, I have learnt how my people-pleasing tendencies were working against me professionally. Identifying how I self-sabotage has been eye-opening. All those times I instinctively said yes or offered to do something outside of my job description, I was gradually losing the respect of my peers by always being available and ready to please. The "more" that I did was never the right type of doing more. Realising this was upsetting and illuminating in equal measure. I now recognise that those succeeding around me were driven by personal success; elevation of their status within the firm and the profession, and wealth. I was not driven in the same way, especially when the competing interest was to be present and available for my daughter. Now that I have a better understanding of what was holding me back, I realise that I want something more than money and status. Of course, both of these things are important and still have a role. However, for me, they only offer short-term satisfaction.

Reaching this point of realisation has been voyage of success and failure, joy and pain, calm and panic, and ultimately self-discovery. There have been reasons for wanting to leave and reasons for wanting to stay in law. The intermittent excitement of the job, the sense of pride I felt from the reaction of others when I told them 'I'm a lawyer', and the promise of job security all play a part in why I stayed for so long.

There are also other elements of the job that kept me in it. I genuinely enjoyed the intellectual challenge of legal research and finding or crafting an answer to a legal problem or question. I took great pride in advising clients on issues arising in their cases in a plain and coherent way without making them feel intimidated or confused, both verbally and in writing. It would also be disingenuous not to mention the many material perks of the job, such as expensing work-related travel and dining, the excuse to always dress well and the many parties. Conversely, there isn't another job or profession pulling me away from law. The absence of anything concrete to work or move towards has provoked feelings of insecurity and fear.

Being a lawyer always deceptively offered me an identity and a sense of belonging to something. A future without that assurance felt unnerving.

I now recognise that what drew me towards law and then kept me there, for the most part, were extrinsic motivations, including social status, prestige and material success. This was a pivotal realisation for me, particularly in understanding why I have not been able to achieve the job satisfaction I crave. It has also forced me to reflect on what is truly important to me.

Becoming a mother made me re-evaluate the time and energy I was investing in my career and accept that I wanted and needed balance. The things that really matter to me are quite basic: self-acceptance, family, friends, secure and content children who grow up to value and recognise their place in the world. I still have a strong sense of wanting to do something meaningful at work and I am sure that with potentially another twenty-five to thirty working years ahead of me, I will. However, I now recognise the value of making decisions with more thought and depth than I have before.

Surprisingly, having left private practice as a lawyer, I have started a new job as a visiting lecturer at the institution where I studied law.

At this stage, I am not committing to a permanent or full-time role. In many ways, I feel as though I am taking the time out now that I think many eighteen-year-olds would benefit from upon finishing school.

In stepping away from the career I had instinctively chosen to please others, for the first time I have shown up as myself. Without the pressure of working in an environment that did not fundamentally suit me, I no longer feel the need to constantly adapt or change to fit in. The perennial disappointment about not quite achieving what I thought I wanted or needed is dissipating.

I can now grow as a more complete version of myself by accepting and integrating the various versions of me that have never come together as one person. The present and the future are no longer about regretting what did not happen or constantly striving for more. Now, with the benefit of my experiences (good and bad) and the self-knowledge I have, I am beginning to feel a sense of freedom. I feel free to choose what I want without the pressures that have weighed upon me from a young age. I feel free to carve out my own place in the world, a place where I belong.

CHAPTER TEN

Life Stories

A RESPONSE TO AMI FROM SUSIE

> Those who do not have power over the story that dominates their lives, power to retell it, to rethink it, deconstruct it, joke about it, and change it as times change, truly are powerless.
>
> Salman Rushdie

I hope that you found Ami's story deeply moving. We can learn so much from what the client chooses to tell and not tell, how they see themselves; hero? Survivor? Victim? I nearly always start my client programmes with listening to their life story. You will always know yourself a bit better when you draw out or tell this story (see reflection exercise below).

This is so relevant when you are exploring your career; who you are and what you do is influenced by the story that you tell yourself. What will shape the content of your own story? How can you believe that you are the author of that story both now and, more importantly, tomorrow?

What got you here, won't get you there

My client, Jamie, sits opposite me, alive with the realities of today and the possibilities of tomorrow. He begins to tell his life story; that collection of memories, perceptions, experiences and beliefs that now give him a platform to explore the future. Drawing out a lifeline has helped Jamie to remember and explore those life-changing events that have shaped his values and beliefs. What are those defining moments for him? When life has been challenging, what has he learnt about himself? What has been the most fulfilling?

Jamie's parents were entrepreneurs; life was bountiful until it wasn't. He explains to me that he grew up with constant financial uncertainty. Jamie had to leave his expensive school and spend his last two years of education in the local sixth form college. He made a decision to work ferociously, getting the grades to study economics and giving himself a passport to financial stability and long-term employability. His early life experiences have meant that this need for security has been at the centre of his career decision making. Jamie has a large house and financial freedom but is now wanting to challenge these life-long motivations and explore how he might define purpose in a different way. Was it fear that kept him in a job that he didn't enjoy for too long? There are many cultural expectations that we want to measure up against and we often try to work hard to do what is expected or will be seen as 'successful'.

Events such as Jamie's can sit so deeply in our unconscious and can guide our decision-making as we become adults. Transactional analysis theorists call this a 'life script'. It is best explained as entrenched childhood decisions that are made unconsciously. They are a response to messages we have been given by parents and the community about ourselves and the world around us. Whilst they might serve us well in childhood, some assumptions made in OUR life script can then become a blocker in adulthood. When we reflect on our lives, we take particular events and then link them into themes. As you read the essays in this book, you will be able to spot the themes that emerge for each writer. What do you think might be the themes that Jamie held before coaching? Diligent worker? Survivor? Provider? Security craver? How much have the decisions that Jamie has taken in his life been informed by this single story? What other experiences and beliefs did Jamie have that might allow him to experiment with new ways of working?

Steven reminisces and reflects about his working life in chapter thirteen. He explores how the recollection of past events is such an imprecise science. Steven's life plan seems to have been mapped, packaged and ready for export. However he begins to reveal that the flow is less steady and we see tiny fault lines breaking along the surface. I imagine my own past as a fleet of small fishing boats, teeming with the day's catch. Each boat represents a part of my life experience. Some vessels are always in my sight, some drift over the horizon, almost imperceptible to me. These boats leave a wash in my mind and I use them to create meaning that is unique to me. But they have also originated from and been developed and maintained by views that are cultivated by the society or the social group I have come from.

We are the stories we tell ourselves

If storytelling seems so fundamental to our being, it's because narrative is so hardwired into our programming that we would lose all sense of identity without it. It's how we create an illusion of a single, cohesive self. It allows individual parts of our life to be connected in a meaningful way.

David Denborough and Nazelo Ncube have created a fascinating exercise, the Tree of Life (i). It is a visual metaphor in which a tree represents your life and the various elements that make it up – past, present, and future. Participants are invited to think of a tree – its roots, trunk, branches, leaves, etc – and imagine that each part of the tree represents something about their life.

REFLECT

Take a piece of paper or use the stylus on your tablet and draw a curvy line across the page which details your career from leaving school until today.

This curvy line will have highs and lows. Take some time to think about what was happening for you in these periods. When were your most fulfilled moments? What are the common themes that link your happiest moments? What might your story tell you about what you are passionate about? When do you feel you are at your very best; that things are going well and somehow you don't have to try too hard because you are being true to yourself? Conversely, what makes you feel so angry, frustrated, or fed up that you feel compelled to act? What are you prepared to stand up for? To be brave about? To stand firm on?

Open up and understand

Joe, 37, is CEO of a small but hugely successful arts company, loved and admired by all around him. He is a straight A student, with a degree from one of the most elite universities. Joe transports himself very quickly back to being eleven years of age, standing at the top of the stairs and overhearing his parents' anxious, concerned conversation. He had failed to get into the academic school that his clever sister had gone to. Plans were being made for him to go elsewhere. The shame he felt stays with him now. Joe explores this with me: 'I still feel that I need to work harder than most in order to produce satisfactory/mediocre work and that those around me who do less work than me, are more capable/naturally intelligent/better than me. Whenever I do not get something right, I take it as another form of proof that I am not good at what I do.' Joe had begun to think that he was the problem and that there was something wrong with him. He takes action against himself; deflecting attention, working ferociously hard behind the scenes, holding back from acting like a leader.

When long-held beliefs about self are questioned they can begin to be challenged. The psychologist Robert Kegan (ii) writes, 'Transformation takes place when we develop the ability to step back and reflect on something that used to be taken for granted yet now enters our consciousness in a way that allows us to make new decisions about it.' It is this transformation that can take place in coaching; the process of taking the time to look at the journey we have been on, hold it up to the light and question long-held assumptions.

REFLECT Question Your Assumptions

Draw three columns on your page and take your time with this exercise, perhaps over a week or two?

Column 1 – Write down every time you watch, read or hear an assumption, judgment or evaluation of what life is about.Add some of the messages you received as a child and young adult in this column too.

Column 2 – Write down every time you could have made an assumption, inference or judgment about what might work in someone else's life, but you DIDN'T

Column 3 – Write down every time you notice yourself thinking about how you might define success which goes against the conventional. Think of three expectations of how you should be that you want to resign from?

Change a little, change a lot

My client, Thomas, grew up in a German provincial town, strongly identifying with German liberal culture as fostered by his parents who were both academics. As a child he was both introverted and shy. Life was about working hard and keeping your head down. Emotions weren't explored or discussed at home. We began to work together when he was 34 and still holding back from sharing more about himself to others. His relationship with his team at work was task-related and transactional. In our sessions together we explored new ways of thinking about himself and the tools he could use to help him connect more with his team.

He arrived to work in China when he was 30 with firmly held scripts about what it was like to "be" German or "be" Asian. He reflects on this work: 'As a foreigner in China, I had a really strong bias to think that what made me successful is that my "German" culture helped to address some needs of the organisation in a better way than what a Chinese employee could have done. You started to convince me to look beyond this limited view, and for the first time, I really could see it.' Thomas and I explored how his values and beliefs had changed and discussed his increasingly deep need to connect with the the individual hopes and fears of his team members.

'Last but not the least,' Thomas says, 'one of my team members remarked near the end of our meeting that our regular team workshop "felt like group therapy". I took this opportunity to share openly a bit more about the struggles I had during my first years in the organisation with no one to really talk to except my boss and that it was sometimes painful to keep all the challenges I had with a customer inside me even if I don't have answers.' Thomas was experimenting with showing more vulnerability than he had previously done and this had a powerful impact on the rest of the team.

These stories illustrate some of those elements of our early lives that become a part of our assumptions and behaviours as adults. It's tough when you begin to challenge long-held beliefs, there is a liminal space where ambiguity and disorientation exist and that feels uncomfortable. Whenever we take a new step in our lives, the voices in our head can become unsettled. You have to be brave enough to experiment with new ways of doing things. Some of the wisest words I have heard are about starting from a point of acceptance about your early life. Those rich experiences have shaped you and made you, you, warts and all. It's now about how you leave behind what is no longer serving you.

We have choice and the ability to build a new sense of who we might become. Setting this all in the context of what you value and care about should sit at the foundation of your thinking. Take a look at chapter four. Victor Frankel, a survivor of the Nazi concentration camps, wrote in his book *Man's Search for Meaning* (iii): 'a human being is not one in pursuit of happiness but in search of a reason to become happy.'

Defining and articulating this very individual sense of purpose is integral to flourishing in your career. Paying attention to when this purpose begins to shift into something different is often a call to make change happen.

CHAPTER ELEVEN

Found On An Engineer's Laptop

JONNY

Some years ago, much to my children's embarrassment, I agreed to help at their school annual prizegiving evening. Introduced on stage as a social entrepreneur, my daughter's super-smart friend whispered, '... that means he doesn't actually have a job.' You could say that. It means I create my own jobs, chart my own course, bring people together, develop new ideas, and try to make interesting or better things happen.

I am driven to improve things. My parents, I suppose, taught me that if I don't change things then nobody else will, and they gave me the security to believe that if I sometimes get it wrong, it is unlikely to be fatal. I am generally inclined to take action, to do something rather than nothing. It's a thrilling but sometimes exhausting way to be, and age and experience lead me to feel a need for balance, to sometimes just accept things just as they are. It doesn't come easily to me though and I am always thinking of new projects, plans and pursuits.

The start of my working life in the mid-1990s coincided with the rise of digitalisation: rapidly advancing computing and communications technologies were being deployed across all parts of society, disrupting, and transforming our world. It has had wonderful and horrendous consequences, in frustratingly equal proportion. Drawn to tackling complexity, and being ambitious, probably over-ambitious, about my capacity to make a difference, led me to want to navigate the challenges and contradictions of digitalisation. Tackling its negative consequences for society whilst championing its many benefits has become the defining theme of my career.

Twenty-five years later, the information superhighway, as it was once called, is an accepted part of everyday life in the global north. It has allowed me and others to keep working, even to prosper, during the pandemic. In my world of work, people have always worked on the move, connecting and collaborating from wherever, whenever. As a telecoms executive I had almost always been on a home-based contract, so meeting people in real life was already an important privilege rather than an everyday expectation. How incredible it is that the internet has eroded physical distance, keeping loved ones connected and children educated. It enables extraordinary access to knowledge and information, and the acceptance of its capabilities by old-fashioned organisations is surely a silver lining to the dark clouds of the early 2020s. Unfortunately, the distribution of these benefits remains very uneven, both within rich countries and across the world.

My very English parents lived in Zambia until I was two years old. My father worked in local government and was helping to set up the post-colonial administration in the copper mining city of Kitwe, where I was born. On their return to England with me, they found an old stone cottage that I still call home, despite all the other homes I have found and created since I was a boy. It has mullioned windows and an amazing view up a valley towards the ridge that marks the edge of the moors at the northern tip of the Dark Peak. The place is beautiful and generally soggy, with rugged and bracing countryside in one direction and post-industrial wasteland in the other. As my parents prospered in public service professions, the country suffered power cuts and strikes, and I enjoyed long summers, Scout night hikes, bikes, and brass banding.

It was an educated, relatively privileged, and left-wing household. My father officiated in elections and smoke-filled committee rooms, and my mother worked in the health service and campaigned for CND. They gave me a respect for public service, an interest in politics and a belief that it is possible to change the world. My first trip to London was on a chartered train to a big anti-nuclear demonstration

91

in 1981. As the protestors protested, my dad took my brother and me onboard *HMS Belfast*, a warship moored in the River Thames. We were all, as a family, profoundly opposed to the Thatcher government and all that it stood for. I grew up to be suspicious of free enterprise and critical of business, which seems an unlikely start for an entrepreneur and business leader.

As a young man I worked in bars, shops and warehouses. I delivered pizza in a van without a reverse gear. Alongside these jobs, I enjoyed creating projects, following my interests and optimistically, sometimes foolishly, making things happen. At school I had produced an edgy magazine, the first edition of which included a cartoon of the building being protected by a giant condom. The caption, 'don't die of ignorance', was taken from the government AIDS awareness campaign, and was a step too far for the head teacher. My English teacher, who didn't normally do much, suddenly came to life and rushed up to me demanding a copy before they were all withdrawn. Of course, there were more editions and then a music fanzine.

The world changed as the Berlin Wall came down, and in 1989 a series of peaceful revolutions opened Central and Eastern Europe to a new wave of globalisation. That year I went off down south, to Sussex University, to study Social Anthropology. I was, and am, interested in how societies, nations and institutions work, and Africa was somehow in my blood, so this seemed the obvious course for me.

At university I made videos, at one point distributing fringe TV programmes on video tape, one cassette delivered to your house for each of the three weeks of the Brighton Festival. We must have used a lot of plastic.

I stayed on at Sussex to complete an MA in Anthropology, exploring material culture and the media. I was interested in the representation of culture in museums and galleries, but also the culture of organisations. It was during this time, in 1993, that the launch of the Netscape web browser sparked the growth of the internet as a huge cultural and commercial phenomenon. I then studied computing at Middlesex University and started to understand the waves and layers of disruption that the internet was bringing to the media industries and saw how transformational it might be. I immersed myself in its development and, with a quaint idea about widening public access, a friend and I reclaimed a derelict building near Brighton seafront and opened a cyber-café. We had a great time, making something from nothing, and bringing a new sparkle to a down-at-heel back street. I learnt about the nuts and bolts of the internet, and something about business, but also quarrelled and lost money.

In the late 1990s, I co-founded an online calendar business. With 20,000 users we took trips to Silicon Valley and New York and developed detailed plans to sell data to advertisers. Our service gathered and stored information about people's next moves, their future intentions. Of course, it was completely free to use, offered in return for the personal information which we planned to sell to advertisers. With better timing and a different location, I might have made a bigger contribution to the internet dominant, and hugely problematic, business model. The pioneers of surveillance capitalism were ahead of us, and anyway clearly didn't need our help. As the 1990s dot com bubble burst, so did mine.

After hearing my story, a recruiter in a café advised me to go and get some 'proper' corporate experience. By the time the planes flew into the twin towers in 2001, I was working in the Covent Garden office of an American cable TV giant, surrounded by TV screens. We checked in with friends in Manhattan as the awful events unfolded, reaching them by email as the phone networks melted down.

The following twenty years saw exciting and terrible developments in digital technology to transform the way ideas spread, democracy functions, and wars are fought. Given my childhood background and education, it was strange to find myself in such a transatlantic and corporate environment. I was surprised to find the people smart and likeable, and enjoyed the challenges of crafting ventures, products, and services. If I was a bit different then I think people put that down to my knowing something about computers.

My managers also appreciated my instinct to act, to keep moving forward in the face of uncertainty and incomplete information. But quiet determination can be mistaken for inaction and inflexibility. I am often imagining, proposing, testing, adapting some new version of the present, some vision of the future, looking for a workaround or a cunning plan. I can arrive in strange and interesting places but sometimes on my own: I learnt that to make progress I must take time to join up the dots, explaining to others how and why I got there.

I continued to do what I have always done: putting together new ideas and pushing to make them happen. Inside a big company it was clearer where investment would come from, but most strikingly it was so much easier to find people who would help and support my cause. I just picked up the phone and talked to unknown colleagues about what I was trying to do, and they wanted to help, apparently without consideration for why they should. It wasn't that I was in charge: we were just all working in the same direction. I also applied my project-starting superpowers, driven by an urge to learn, create, and cut through complexity, and empowered as an intrapreneur within a matrix structure. Not that I understood that at the time. We were delivering the first domestic broadband internet services, something I had been dreaming of: if you've moved house recently you may have been reminded of how important this has become. It means there are messages and video calls, shopping, films and games, instant access to banks, books, music, photographs and more. Obviously. But until the turn of the century that was all new.

Like other big infrastructure developments, the British cable industry went bust more than once, and working for a bankrupt company wasn't comfortable. The chairman publicly fell out with the CEO and they both walked the floor, quite aggressively trying to motivate people. They missed the opportunities of surveillance capitalism, or were structurally prevented from pursuing it. Likely a bit of both. All that is solid melts into air: when I started working in the mobile business, I was given a Blackberry, the handheld email device and business tool of choice for a few years before the iPhone arrived.

Sometimes people say that I am, or was, ahead of events. I've often had visions for new projects and creations, but not so explicitly for myself. I never imagined becoming an entrepreneur, a leader, or even a father in very much detail. These things didn't happen because of what I wanted to be but because of what I was trying to do: create a product, make change happen, have a family. Explaining what I do always seems to be complicated: for instance, I am not an engineer, but I am sometimes mistaken for one. Once, on a crime report, the police insisted on writing that a 'BT engineer's laptop' had been stolen. There isn't really a simple answer, and at the time that was near enough, so I accepted the compliment.

You could say that I am a first-generation digital parent: my daughters were born into a doom-scrolling culture that is not yet at peace with the might of its machines. Our family home in London was in large part financed by the mobile phone industry, an industry that did such a good job of not marketing to children that within twenty years of its inception it was serving nearly every eleven-year-old. In my early thirties, the meeting rooms at my office proclaimed the company values: bold, open, trusted, clear. For a long time, my contribution was evaluated in these terms, so it has surely shaped how I work. I juggled my family, work, and the demands of an Executive MBA which was an important training but, like my earlier post-graduate study in computer science, offered only a very narrow view of the world. Some management students are now taught about the social impact of business models and the key role of ethical business culture, a change that is now urgent, for environmental as well as social and cultural reasons.

In 2003 I was asked to lead a project on the risks to children and young people of new mobile services: significant investments were at stake if networks were unable to properly control the 'girls, games and gambling', the apparent drivers for the adoption of 3G mobile content services. Controlling online content was very much against the zeitgeist and remains politically and technically challenging. I found it interesting and challenging to seek out tactical and strategic solutions, countering claims that it was simply impossible, as well as philosophically wrong. The resistance was wearing, but over the course of seven years or so I delivered on a mission that was strongly aligned with the long-term interests of the company, our society, and my own young family. I enjoyed the creative and leadership challenges of product development and strategic communications but also had a strong personal interest. It turned out that the company, a mobile challenger, was way ahead of the fixed-line incumbents as well as its peers across the world. Importantly, we delivered on a model of corporate social responsibility in which organisations invest to ensure that their core activities achieve positive social impact, as opposed to funding philanthropic projects as cover for more damaging behaviour.

At Tegensee, in the mountains outside Munich, I attended a meeting of corporate responsibility managers from across six European operating businesses. We discussed the importance of trust in our company's services and how it was engendered. It was the start of my big idea to drive group-wide action on digital confidence. By 2010 I had established myself in a new leadership role on this theme. Over breakfast in a boutique hotel in Luxembourg, I agreed with colleagues how we would align efforts across the six European countries in which we operated. It was an internal movement for change around which I convened business leaders from Prague, Bratislava, Munich, Dublin, London, Brussels and Madrid. Good times: my company was a market leader and had recently been acquired. It reoriented me around southern Europe: an exciting place to visit, a new language to learn and another culture to explore. I was energised and enriched by working with so many talented people from so many different places. I was engaged with the British government and regulators, but more interesting for me, with the European Commission and its networks of safer internet awareness centres and of hotlines for illegal content.

Over the years, colleagues have insisted that it is impossible to establish which users are children, or to filter out pornographic, violent, or other harmful content. It is often considered too difficult to disrupt the distribution of child abuse images, to put users in control of how their data is used, to stop scams or the spread and amplification of lies and hate online. Yet those organisations that have tried have gone a long way towards achieving both. As part of my company's work in this field, I supported the work and development of a charity that seeks to eliminate child sexual abuse online. I became the mobile sector representative and in 2010 was elected to the charity's board. I served six years as the industry vice-chair, recruiting for key leadership roles, developing strategy, and building my experience of non-profit and charity governance. The board valued my industry knowledge and creative thinking and together we developed important new strategies and expanded operations from the UK to twenty-five countries across the world. It was a fantastic opportunity for me as a company executive to apply my corporate influencing experience, gain non-executive experience, and better understand the problem of online images of child abuse.

In 2012, after careful planning and quite a bit of luck, my wife and I were both seconded to work in Brussels. From early in my career, if not in my education, I had been caught up in the European project. The Channel Tunnel opened when I was 24. Before that I took the Virgin Express plane from Gatwick to Brussels to work on projects in the European Strategic Programme on Research in Information Technology. When it arrived, I preferred the train, speeding through northern France and Flanders to Brussels with coffee and a croissant or watching the sun set with a beer in the buffet car on the way home to London. Nearly twenty years later, living on the doorstep of the European Institutions for the first time, meeting daily with lobbyists, EU officials and politicians brought me a new level of knowledge and understanding European Affairs.

The Snowden revelations and a review of the European data protection rules added urgency to my corporate mission to establish clear internal policies on privacy, safety and security, as a foundation for a more trusted Internet and a leading digital business. I still faced resistance from engineers and others, a resistance that is aligned with the misdirected culture of big tech that was laid bare by the Facebook-Cambridge Analytica data scandal when it finally broke in 2018. Why didn't the kings of Silicon Valley see how they were getting it so badly wrong? Changing professional culture was and is no easy task. My main strategy, which worked but too slowly, was to

97

establish an internal programme and then persuade the most senior leaders of the company to speak about it externally.

Smart, data-driven digital technologies automate everything, making energy, transport, and healthcare infrastructure more effective, efficient and available. They optimise our time but also waste our time. The divide between us and the other half of the world's population, the 3.7 billion that are without internet connectivity, has become deeper and sharper during the pandemic. For those who are lucky enough to be included in the digital world, cultural and political difference has turned violent as lies and abuse are amplified. Everything we do leaves a footprint by which daily life is encoded and traded as part of a complex, data-driven economy. Too often, for me and many others I think, all this can distract and reduce the quality of relationships. People become both more, and very much less, connected. For me, and I am sure for others, the pandemic put a stop to some critical face to face meetings. Whilst I've achieved a lot by Zoom, there is a limit. Difficult conversations are still more difficult without the chance to talk in person.

When organisations take a wrong turn, as some big tech companies have done, it can be masked by impressive management processes as well as good but misguided people. At university, the anthropologists taught me to look beyond the internal logic of technologies, systems, and organisations, to attend to the ways in which people shape and reshape them, and the reasons that they do it. I've come to believe that a deep understanding of, and engagement with, organisational culture is an important part of corporate accountability and the key to the development of ethical business practice. This can help organisations to understand and address the negative social consequences of their activities before it is too late.

We had six years back in London before recently returning to live in Brussels. During that time, I joined the Governing Boards of two secondary schools. As a parent I had an interest in understanding how things worked, but my commitment was more about learning and service. Sitting on panels I heard really difficult staffing and student behaviour cases which opened my eyes to the community I lived in and took me out of my professional comfort zone. I had the opportunity to contrast my working life as a leader in a multinational corporation with that of school leaders in two quite different inner city state schools. One, an improving inclusive community school with a rapidly increasing staff morale, the other, a failed school in the process of a bungled rescue by a well-intentioned academy trust. Despite big differences of approach, they had one big thing in common before the pandemic: they refused to recognise the importance of all young people having access to their own, connected computer. Some leaders said that students just didn't need computers of their own. Others objected that if children were given laptops, they would be taken by their families and sold. When schools were closed in March 2020, some leaders blamed the low take-up of online learning on a lack of motivation on the part of the students. What planet were they on?

The pandemic highlighted the extent to which children in wealthy countries must compete with others in their own household for basic digital access. Of the eleven million people in the UK who do not use a computer, a rising proportion are young people who are only counted as Internet users because they access social media apps. Both the army and the construction industry are struggling with new recruits who don't know the basics of using a computer. It is extraordinary that the businesses that have the greatest interest in children's digital literacy, those that are also the richest companies in the world, have allowed such a socially divisive situation to escalate. This must be put right: it is really very important that every young person should have a connected laptop, of their own.

I am focused on the transformative possibilities of global corporations because I think this is a critical lever to achieve social change. It must be possible to genuinely adjust the motivation of big organisations to value innovation, profit, but also positive social impact. The single-minded focus on short-term shareholder value, traditionally taught at business school and deeply embedded in the culture of most big businesses, is bad for investors, for organisations, for people and for society. It led to a wrong turn in Silicon Valley twenty years ago, when the Internet adopted a business model based on gathering and exploiting personal data. The next twenty years will be the second part of my career: who knows how it will turn out, but my first idea is to contribute to a new direction for the next twenty years of digital development, starting with more European values and with my current work with big online businesses to review how they are tackling online hate, harm, and abuse. My life as a social entrepreneur has shifted dramatically since those early years and no doubt will shift again as society changes.

CHAPTER TWELVE

Is the Concept of Career Dead?

A RESPONSE TO JONNY FROM SUSIE

> The only skill that will be important in the twenty-first century is the skill of learning new skills. Everything else will become obsolete over time.
>
> Peter Drucker

When I was a child, I would often be at a playdate with a carriage clock. Often gold-plated. Carriage clocks were often given as retirement presents and many of my friends' parents would proudly display the clock that had been given to their grandparent. The clock was a timely representation of a working life spent mostly in one organisation. Today the picture is dramatically different. In 2022, one in four people in the UK have been in their job for less than a year.

In fact, a UK worker will change employer every five years on average, according to research by life insurance firm, LV (ii). In the US, it's even shorter, with people staying with a single employer for just over four years. Many more of us are extending our education and rethinking traditional ideas and stereotypes of what a career might look like. This is primarily in response to massive economic, technological and societal changes. The pandemic launched a final giant demolition hammer at our twentieth-century notion of career and the idea that we must be present in the office 24/7.

The way we work is changing, but it is possible to set yourself up for success in the decades to come. A job today is much more than a way to earn money; it's a way for us to be creative, learn new skills, take risks and make a difference. This emphasis on self-exploration and improvement has meant many individuals are always looking to be "better" and see the relationship with their employer as somewhat transactional. They want fast growth, and they won't stick around at the same company to find it. Today, professionals take their career into their own hands, figure out their own story, and move around to create the right career path for them. It's now easier than ever to find a new job. Instead of going to a recruitment agency or looking in a newspaper, you can go online and apply for jobs in just a few clicks. Governments are pushing back workers' standard retirement age. Fewer of us are now able to retire after thirty years.

Jonny's story is interesting because he harnessed technology to create new businesses; remember his first internet calendar business back in the 1990s? But he has also sat alongside the digital revolution and witnessed its transformative power, both its benefits and its more pernicious impact. Jonny is also a great example of somebody who has spiralled around in his career, holding onto the digital theme but exploring it in both small businesses, start-ups, large corporates and latterly a think tank.

So, do we know what jobs will matter – or even exist – in the future?

I reflect on roles that didn't exist when I was growing up. Sophie, who is 32, is an environmental expert and works for a Green Bank. Green Banks are mission-driven institutions that use innovative financing to accelerate the transition to clean energy and fight climate change. Sophie heads up employee engagement and stewardship and tells us, 'I'm continuing to build on the engagement work that my organisation has done on issues such as climate change, modern slavery and health and nutrition. The unprecedented scale of the sustainable development challenges we face will require a bold shift in stewardship practices over the next decade.'

We all recognise that the climate emergency is creating new types of job opportunities, but there are now also broader development challenges needing to be worked through, as Sophie recognises. Sustainability is a real priority for all type of organisations and businesses. The challenge for many is how to run a business that looks after the planet without sacrificing profitability. This includes areas such as diversity and inclusion, social enterprise and crisis management. I work alongside many people rethinking their career choices because of the existential threat of climate change.

Sophie worked for a traditional investment bank after university. After searching for greater impact in her work and a recognition of the massive opportunities available in the green sector, she stepped away to study for a Master's in environmental technology. She was then able to leverage her work and education to begin her career in the green sector.

Jonny was, and still is, focused on both harnessing and improving the way digitalisation facilitates and impacts our lives. Computer and information technology operations are predicted to grow in the UK by 13% between 2020 and 2030, and the fast growth means that salaries are also rising more quickly than in most other industries. Two blossoming areas are cybersecurity and healthcare technology.

Milicia, 43, had a tough time during the Covid pandemic. As a rising star in her global retail organisation, she had been promoted over five years from retail assistant to sales and operations director for Eastern Europe. Sales collapsed during the pandemic and the company was not able to survive. She had always been adept at using innovative data in retailing and was also aware of the increasing threat of cybercrime. Milicia used her redundancy to retrain as a cybersecurity technician. She is now in the final stages of interviewing with a global consulting group.

Grace has understood the power of technology in changing people's lives since she was a small girl growing up in a family of engineers. She always had the long-term goal of building and scaling her own solutions to a social issue. She built great foundations by working both for global technology companies but also other start-ups, before she felt ready to start her own company. Grace founded a digital health behaviour change service which helps individuals to keep on top of mental and physical health through small achievable habits. The organisation is currently scaling across NHS primary care practices and with local authorities, and has supported over 20,000 members of the public to date. Remarkably she is only 32. Grace needs technical expertise but also must run projects, design, manage client relationships and build her team.

If only this was easy

Making a big career change is daunting. We all recognise one of those first questions when we meet somebody new: 'So what do you do?' The writers in this book give powerful accounts of what works means to them but also the challenge to their sense of self when making a career shift. Work can define who we are and anchor ourselves to some sort of stability. What if you switch careers and fail? What is your identity then? We think of career as something we are building over time. It can give us the chance to feel good about how we have progressed. But if we change career how will we apply what we have learnt? Will we be able to carry it with us? What happens if our new career makes us less money? Should we continue if we still enjoy it? Or do something different?

Riding the wave

While many technical skills are in high demand, they decrease in value as more people acquire capability in those skills. How could you upskill right now?

As I write this piece, artificial intelligence is not only revolutionising the way that work is carried out in organisations, it's becoming readily available to us all with the launch of chatbots. By 2039, approximately 4.5 million new STEM jobs will be created globally, including engineers, scientists, IT and digital professionals, economists, statisticians, and teachers. These are important skills for the future but so is the ability to be emotionally intelligent, think critically, research and have writing skills.

Be intentional, find a mentor, and set goals

Starting out on a new career path or building a business doesn't come easily of course. It's natural to be fearful. Take a look back at chapter two to help you here. If you're intentional and seek out realistic roles at companies, you can learn and grow. A mentor can help you achieve your goals of finding success in your new career. Take a look at chapter eighteen here – Relationships Are the Source of Results. Setting clear measurable goals will allow you to challenge yourself but also remember that there will be much experimentation and learning along the way. You never really know what you can make happen until you actually give yourself the space and opportunity to do so.

I look at Eliza's working life. It seems to be typical of a Gen Z. Still in her mid-twenties, Eliza is a freelancer, a "hustler" or digital nomad and constantly searches for ways to be both creative and find meaningful work. She really wants to turn her passion into full-time work and the idea of a nine to five office job is a real anathema. Taking her interest in love, sex and relationships as a central theme of her work, she uses this in a variety of freelance guises. These include an online curated community forum, training as a relationship coach, producing a poetry book, copy and content writing. Social media facilitates all the work that she does and allows her to monetise her work. Life feels less secure, but Eliza is continually learning, building new relationships and able to quickly shift direction when needed. She is her own boss, which for her feels liberating, but she needs to be a powerful leader of her own life in order to make this sort of career choice succeed. But life feels less secure for her anyway; past generations could work hard, buy a house and afford a decent standard of living. This feels untenable for her and many of her generation.

Two thirds of professionals under the age of 24 claim to have a 'side hustle', with 74% stating it is 'too risky' to focus on just having one job as they may have done pre-pandemic. Some of my clients have a small business that sits alongside their main job. Felix has an online- fashion business. He sources clothes in the UK, rebranding and styling them for target consumer groups. He talks about how it has developed his self-discipline, finance skills, social media and marketing expertise and ability to be organised.

Future proofing questions to ask yourself

→ What's happening in my sector; where is the growth, where do things look more vulnerable?

→ What's my current relationship with technology?

→ Am I understanding how to collaborate with people from different industries and different walks of life?

→ How can my network better support your growth?

→ Who needs to know that I am seeking new career growth experiences?

→ Am I up for new ways of learning?

→ Am I open to new ideas?

→ Do I have a realistic idea of my abilities and what they are worth?

→ What skills and work environments give me energy and bring out the best in me?

How can the organisations that you are part of build career models that encourage continuous learning, improve individual mobility, and foster a growth mind-set in every employee, year after year? This is the opportunity for today; companies that figure this out will out-perform, out-innovate, and out-execute their peers. Employers should help prepare and guide their employees though their working lives in which they learn, work, learn, work and cycle through many career stages.

Set against the backdrop of massive societal changes, how will you navigate your way through your working life? A continual process of reflection and experimentation seems to be a good recipe for career right now, along with a healthy dose of keeping up to date with sector change or even being part of this change yourself.

CHAPTER THIRTEEN

Autumn Tapestry

STEVEN

We were having lunch at an outdoor cafe, opposite the glorious gothic architecture of Salisbury Cathedral. Rain and a cold breeze punctuated the conversation. I had known Peter since the start of secondary school. I was the best man at his wedding. I had known his wife, Alison, as long as he had, since we were 16 years old and met up at one of those "let's twin the local all-boys' school with the local all-girls' school for theatre trips and school discos" events, which somewhat dates me.

Alison had recently been told that she had only a few months left to live – she had an aggressive brain tumour and the treatment had finally stopped working. We found ourselves reminiscing, over lunch, about our lives, the world of work and the careers that we had followed. Alison suddenly piped up: 'I haven't told the stories I wanted to!' It was a very upsetting moment, but also challenged my thinking about my own stories and what they might mean, as I was writing this account of my career.

A few years back, when her cancer was first diagnosed, Alison put together her journals and created a wonderful set of photo books of her life. I was fascinated to see where our lives had intertwined and how she perceived those moments, contrasted to my own memories – the same, but with different details and with nuances that I had forgotten. She also started researching her Victorian and Edwardian relatives and writing wonderful biographical histories, of strong, forgotten women. An image that has stayed with me is that of a dovecote – which Alison used as a metaphor for our ancestors, generations jostling against each other, forgotten rooms, dust and detritus and the layers of lives and stories that lead to one another, and to our own lives.

We all have different perspectives of time. Personally, I tend to rush through the present, often fear or over-anticipate the future, and love the past – knitting or embroidering it, so as to make sense of the present. Well into my thirties, I had a very linear view of both time and careers. With intent, willpower and sheer hard work, I believed that I could create a clear path, forwards. This linear thinking was severely jolted, in my early forties – the first, but not last, time that I was made redundant (due to a corporate "restructuring") and again, a couple of years later, when I decided to separate from my then wife of twenty years. Up to that time, I had imagined my "story" to be immutable, that the narrative of our own past lives was, of course, fixed. But then I realised, with a burst of freedom and rewriting my own "scripts" (often through the quasi-therapy of writing poetry) that our own stories are like a kaleidoscope – the pieces and colours all remain the same, but one twist and the patterns look so completely different – as with Alison's journals. And, as for linear – I am learning that we cannot control the course of our careers – we can try to steer, take advantage of opportunities, but failures and detours inevitably occur and need to be absorbed and brought into the story rather than feared. I am starting to realise that it is all part of "becoming" the extraordinary tapestry of who I am today. I understand that slightly better now ... but not then and not for a long time.

Strangely, as I write this, in my early sixties, I find myself in transition again, as I was in my early career – this time into a "portfolio" collection of consulting and coaching projects. A large chunk of my work-life, from my mid-thirties to mid-fifties, was a deliberate attempt at a logical (and ascending) "career" through the corporate world. It did not always lead where I imagined – for both better and worse. Let us start at the beginning, though, to make my story easier to follow.

I was the first family member to go to university. My parents had no clue about careers and I didn't receive much help from anyone else. All I knew was that I wanted to *travel*. It was a recession, in 1981, and there were very few jobs on offer. A major Hong Kong-based bank had an international management graduate scheme and I liked the idea. I submitted my application, in person, to the security guard at the glass and steel London headquarters, at 10pm on the night of the deadline. In the end, it was the only job that I was offered and, after a summer of eating lettuce sandwiches, with debts and no money, I of course took the job.

And so, in the haphazard way that many careers seem to emerge, I went into international retail financial services and I travelled – living in seven different places within the space of eight years. In the 1980s, there was also a different view of careers – that you joined a big organisation, potentially for life. The flexibility and choice of start-ups, freelance careers and the now accepted concept of moving around, in order to advance, barely existed at that time. With seeking to work overseas, I do often wonder whether I was unconsciously (or consciously) escaping my claustrophobic and unhappy childhood, as well as the sort of stifling middle-class Britain that has inspired writers and rock stars (like David Bowie) to escape, in their cases, into creative rebellion. Or, maybe, I just have the "wanderlust" gene? There was also precedent though – my parents had a real curiosity about the world and were open to new experiences and engendered that curiosity in me.

Whichever way, place has been a significant component of my working and adult life. It has often been the reason that I left or stayed in jobs. I have loved the travel adventures, the different cultures and exploration, the sheer, wild beauty of many parts of our planet, and the fellow humanity – discovering that we are all the same, but infinitely different. It has helped me better understand otherness – often being the only person like me in the room and frequently the only native English speaker, and it has helped me to appreciate alternative perspectives. All of which has supported my career and which also now provides a strong base for one of my current new "plural" roles, as an executive coach.

My teenage self would be most surprised, I think, by the fact that I have lived all over the world – across twelve countries and four continents and travelled so widely, literally, millions of miles. Until I left university at the age of 23, I had lived and studied in a narrow 30-mile corridor along the Thames Valley, in south-east England.

Since then, I have lived and worked in places that I had never heard of – Djibouti, the Solomon Islands – as well as some that I already knew, such as Brussels and Paris. Others were just textbook pictures and monochrome assumptions, like Moscow and Johannesburg. With my first, international bank employer, I was eventually sent to the headquarters in Hong Kong and, overall, I have lived there, on and off, for over fourteen years. Asia has become a second home for me, although it would take me another whole chapter to discuss the concept of "home".

After eight years working at the international bank, at the age of 30, having moved countries numerous times and with two small daughters, I decided to leave my steady banking job and do a Master's in Business Administration (MBA) at INSEAD Business School, near Paris. I had started to realise that my undergraduate degree in French and Philosophy did not help me have much understanding of how businesses really work and I felt handicapped in pursuing roles such as marketing. It was a calculated but high-risk shift, to take a year out, with a young family, but I had a good friend as an exemplar, who had just finished at INSEAD and helped me understand the experience. I have not been fortunate enough to have senior mentors during my working life, but I have often found it helpful to calibrate my career and my next steps with how friends or peers have gone through their own working lives. This has certainly been a way for me to explore possibilities and cope with the different paths and risks of my own career changes.

Business school was also meant to be a way to reinvent myself and escape – this time from financial services. I had decided that I wanted to leave banking to join the sort of companies that, if I were to completely rewind the "story", I thought I now wanted to be part of – fast-moving consumer goods companies such as Procter & Gamble or L'Oréal – which were seen, at the time, to be creative and exciting places to work. With eight years of banking background though, I made little headway in applying for such roles.

To compensate for my lackadaisical job search at university, I went all out for jobs in my final months at INSEAD – dozens of job interviews, leading to a handful of job offers. I took the one that kept me overseas and which, in a taste of things to come, was the strangest job interview of my life. I met my final interviewer for just over an hour in the transit lounge at Frankfurt airport. I spent the day travelling to Charles de Gaulle airport then flying between Paris and Frankfurt and back again, not stepping a foot outside Frankfurt airport. And so, that is how my consulting career and a couple of years living in New Zealand and Australia came about.

The experience also allowed for a short, definitive escape from financial services, when a head-hunter lured me from consulting into a strategy role at a major hotel chain. I spent four years in the hospitality industry, across Europe and Asia – "travel" in its very essence. I loved the job, having the opportunity to stay in amazing hotels in places like Bali, Kathmandu or the Whitsundays in Australia. However, my hotel adventures came to an end after the arrival of a new CEO and a major reorganisation. I was offered a compensatory move from Hong Kong to Prague. My eldest daughter had already been to seven different primary schools, so we decided to stay in Hong Kong and rejected the opportunity.

As I now comprehend, this was a significant jolt and watershed to my concept of career – the first time that I had decided to stay in a place rather than leave and, as a result, I was made redundant. It was very difficult for me not to feel that I had lost control of my career and somehow failed. I now realise that this perspective came from the "script" of my messy childhood. My father's army mentality meant that everything at home had to be perfectly shipshape, neat and ordered, to meet his highly exacting demands. If not, there was trouble. And then there was the unpredictable chaos, frequently, when he came home, drunk from the pub, and we had the lightning storms and physical rains of blows. I think desiring order and certainty has not only been instilled into me, but is also a way for me to feel safe, when uncertainty in my childhood was always so deeply unsafe.

There is a psychological theory that the structure of corporate life and work is a way to manage our anxieties and the corporate world has certainly helped serve that purpose for me. Having also seen my father unemployed for long periods, I was petrified of not having a job or money. I started working at the age of 12 – newspaper rounds, graduating to working in a shop, then dishwashing in a pub – to be able to buy myself new clothes, instead of wearing old hand-me-downs from kind friends' parents or my grandmother. A structured corporate career, with a monthly paycheck, allowed me to overcome a visceral fear of having no money. So, losing my hotel industry job led to high anxiety. With a young family to support, I needed to find a next job, quickly. After trying and failing to stay in the travel business, which had few senior roles in Asia, I finally found myself back at another international bank, fulfilling our family goal to stay in Hong Kong.

At times, I have regretted the fact that I was unable to leave banking entirely but, in retrospect, I have found great enjoyment, challenge and purpose in retail financial services. Whatever your view may be of banks or payments companies, they empower individuals and businesses through helping money multiply and flow. I much enjoy understanding customers' views on managing their own money. I also enjoyed the opportunity to lead teams from my early twenties – my first such role being holiday cover for the manager of eight Indian staff in a dusty bank branch, on the outskirts of Abu Dhabi. They spoilt this young Westerner with home-made onion bhajis for lunch – a heart-warming experience. The teams that I managed grew over time and became more complex. It is an aspect of corporate life that I have always relished – helping create a future picture of what we are doing, working together with a team to find solutions and celebrating when we achieved what we had agreed, together – a joint endeavour.

My childhood experiences have also left me with a strong desire to help others and for equality and justice. That seems to have manifested itself in my spending a large chunk of my banking career trying to improve the products or service that we provided to our customers. I think a higher purpose of making sure that customers are fairly and properly treated and served has very much motivated me and kept me connected to financial services throughout my career. Strangely too, as a technology business, retail banking has turned out to be constantly evolving and, with the digital age, is now being disrupted in completely new ways. In the early twenty-first century, in my late-life portfolio career, I currently work part-time with a cryptocurrency start-up – money taken to its digital frontier. I sometimes look back in sheer amazement that, when I started my banking career, I worked in places where they had massive typewriter-like accounting machines (not even computers) and now everything is available in an app, on a mobile phone, and significant chunks of technology are simply invisible.

Staying in Hong Kong with my new banking employer turned out to be a good decision. I managed to gain some very supportive senior management sponsorship – an element that has made a huge difference to my desire to influence and change things for the better, within any company. I love to see businesses (and people) grow and flourish. The new bank was also one of the few workplaces that, for me, also fulfilled another need. I want work to be "family" – the warm, inclusive family that I did not have as a child. Freud talks about how we try, throughout life, to heal the "primal wound" which, of course, is impossible. I came close – in creating my own family with my two daughters and at my new workplace. I helped create and then led a large technology change programme. For four years, it felt like being on the winning sports team – we created positive changes to the lives of staff and customers, we respected our complementary skills and personalities and really enjoyed working with each other; we socialised on a Friday night and at weekends. The stars aligned. Many of those fellow workers became close friends.

It was a special and rare experience for me. More often than not, unfortunately, the transactional (and toxic) nature of many modern organisations has left me disappointed – looking for intimacy and personal fulfilment in the wrong group, the wrong place and discovering that work is just "work" inside many organisations.

Despite enjoying my role and projects at the bank, it was also around this time that I separated from my first wife. Over a couple of years, after meeting hundreds of people during any holiday time back in the UK, I finally gained a senior retail banking role and moved back from Hong Kong. The company culture, at the UK bank I joined, was fairly "tribal" and managers were expected to be loud and assertive – all very different from my Asian-accumulated collaborative style and international outlook. The job turned out to be just a "bridge" back to my birth country.

After a year, I applied for another role, from an advert that, by sheer chance, I had spotted in a Sunday national newspaper, a form of job recruitment that has been completely replaced by Linked In and the internet. Some months later I was living and working in London, for the very first time in my life, now working for a US-headquartered payments company. I had responsibilities across a wide geography. There was lots of travel to the Middle East, Africa and Eastern Europe – many new countries and new discoveries of people, culture and food. I loved the management team that I had joined; a democratic woman leader, a shared purpose of empowering emerging markets through payments and, in the London office, staff from over twenty different countries. I felt "at home" again. Unfortunately, the company was restructured (that word repeated) a number of times and much of the strong, bonding ethos was lost. In late 2009, I was sent, without being asked, to Moscow on temporary assignment, as General Manager for the regional business. I found out from an all staff email when on holiday! The "temporary" lasted three Russian winters and almost four years.

In Moscow, with no personal life, living apart from my new wife, whom I had met just as I was leaving Hong Kong, I gave everything to my work – long hours and six-day weeks. I slipped into familiar old patterns. That was when my blood pressure blew up.

A pattern that has been apparent to me, for some time, is that work is where I have looked, and still look, for validation or recognition. Many people do. During my chaotic childhood, I was only ever rewarded (and not punished) when I did well at school. So, my model or "script" was that, to be loved in any way, I had to work, hard. As early as my mid-twenties, I had collapsed at work from exhaustion and ended up in an ambulance, being rushed to the American Hospital in Paris. Now, in 2013, on a business trip to Kazakhstan, I found myself unable to walk, ended up in the local SOS clinic and was diagnosed with severe hypertension. I need to take the blood pressure pills for the rest of my life.

Eventually, after four years, my assignment in Moscow came to an end. In the previous twelve months, over one hundred of my colleagues had lost their jobs, as the London headquarters had been closed. The end of the assignment, when it arrived, was brutal. The newly appointed CEO had removed most of the previous leadership. He represented a certain school of management which believes that change is best enacted through throwing the past away and bringing in your "own people" rather than using the best of what already exists. The footballing equivalent might be Jose Mourinho – the "wrecker", as compared to Alex Ferguson, the "builder". Over latte and Russian porridge, I was told to pack my bags, leave the next day and not talk to any staff or customers, otherwise all my end of assignment benefits would be removed. I was terminated, with immediate effect. In Jungian terms, this was a "falling upwards" moment when a significant shock breaks our paradigms and leads to new paths. It was against all my values and destroyed my confused and emotionally entwined concepts of work and identity. But as the new CEO had also said to me pointedly at one stage – we are simply "custodians" at work!

Yes, I enjoyed all the challenges and intensity, the adrenaline rush of corporate leadership – managing large budgets and large numbers of people, making "big" decisions, having an important title. I am also, somehow, adept at the corporate game – I enjoy and seem good at synthesising and understanding complex problems and seeing solutions. I can be a clear and warm communicator, setting a vision that others want to follow and I believe in strong collaboration, trusting my teams and helping them grow. Conversely, I hate the politics and hypocrisy and lack of care of many large multi-national corporates.

Work is, nonetheless, a huge part of our human identity and it has been for me. It has given me a context, community, reward, meaning. Organisations have also been a way for me to contain my existential anxieties and provide certainty of task and income, as well as a broad canvas on which to use my skills. I now realise, however, that the way in which I have approached my own work identity has also had major flaws. I have wrapped up such a significant part of my identity

115

in work and neglected or suppressed other identities. I now started to realise that the corporate world is just one part of society and its own significant "bubble". I could no longer define myself just by work, particularly in an age when the social contract between employers and employees is broken and workers have become an economic commodity. I had let my role as provider over-ride many of my and others' needs. I had been an absent father, often on business trips, missing school plays and concerts. Although in my early career, I enjoyed amateur dramatics, community sports and newly learnt hobbies such as pottery, I had become "too busy" for any such balancing interests.

If I could therefore completely rewind my "script", I would want to ensure that I invested more of my time in my non-work identities and better balanced my personal life. There is time still. It was when I was trying to work out my next career steps, after this painful termination experience, that I engaged Susie as a career coach. We went through my life story, what motivated me and what held me back. I was still not completely ready though to break my "scripts" and, in the way that I always had, I planned and networked and interviewed and found myself another role in a business services organisation – leading the consulting practice across Europe. The psychologist who did my recruitment assessment astutely saw that a major shift had started. The scores on a number of my standard behavioural tests had changed from previous years. I no longer came out as so structured and task-driven, inflexible. Instead, scores around caring, intuition and creativity had risen significantly. Was this a result of the shock of "falling upwards" or had this always been a part of me and I had simply suppressed that side of my character, in order to fit the expectations of others? He challenged as to why I was continuing with corporate life. Why, indeed?

I found the job in my new company very lonely and unfulfilling. I was the only person in my team in London. I spent all my time on conference calls and lacked all the essential social aspects of work life. As an outcome from my reflections and a suggestion from Susie, I looked at training as an executive coach and did a part-time Master's in Executive Coaching, while still working. Again, I was using education as a way to reinvent myself, in the same way that I had done at INSEAD. Coaching and mentoring were an experiment, which seemed to have no downside. The worst outcome would be that I might become a better leader. It turned out that I loved it – understanding others, listening, helping them reflect, seeing myself in them and, sometimes, gently guiding them away from the errors that I felt that I had made. Although, of course, we all need to make our own, same mistakes to learn; it is the way that the human brain is wired.

So, after thirty-six years of corporate life, I jumped from my full-time role to become freelance. My workmates told me how I brave I was – a way to hide that they thought I was foolish to leave the emotional and material containment of corporate life? Or jealousy? Or genuine observation?

A good friend of mine says that we don't all live life in the same order. Some of us are always in, say, a "steady" middle-aged decade, others live their decades in a progressive and developmental order. I feel that I am now living the start of my adulthood in a way that I did not permit myself at the time – now a little wiser and certainly more affluent. I am also trying to reframe, to think of this uncertain mess as something more organic – like reeds and lilies in a pond, with dragonflies flitting above the surface – as opposed to my preference for a symmetric, modern building, with rectilinear scaffolding. I am also discovering that the nature of portfolio life means work continuously shifts and changes. Equally, I am finding that to gain projects or roles, I need to write and rewrite my career story all the time, to make any sense in new worlds.

After almost four years of this portfolio career, I am still held by some of my old patterns. I have joined and left a coaching company where I tried to find another "family", but instead only discovered a team of lone-wolf individuals who were focused on maximising their own earnings. My need to be "busy" in order to manage my anxieties, and the resultant, seemingly opportunistic projects that I am involved in, seems messy and unfocused to me. Or maybe they are explorations and that is the way we find the identities that we have inside us, but don't yet know or understand. I am trying to integrate my corporate experience with relational and humanistic perspectives. I have a wide range of current roles: at the time of writing, on the board of an international bank subsidiary; advising a fintech start-up; on the board of a cultural data and technology company (which has been a way for me to stay involved in the arts), and in a wide range of mentoring and coaching networks, often involved with diversity, supporting women and minority ethnic leaders.

As the philosopher Kierkegaard noted: 'Life can only be understood backwards; but it must be lived forwards.' Looking back at my story, there have been some big themes in my personal and work life: place; safety; workaholism; seeking a substitute family through work life; the contrasting cognitive and creative parts of my personality, which I have never fully balanced. I have come to appreciate Carl Jung's thinking on the stages of our lives. He saw the early phases as a time to build our families and careers and to create a necessary "ego". Then, in our final decades – our "autumn years" – we have the opportunity to let go of that "ego", give back to others and integrate all parts of ourselves.

My current quest, in my post-corporate portfolio career, of many diverse projects and roles, seems to be that elusive search for integration of my different identities. Helping young leaders in start-ups to understand themselves and create sustainable businesses seems to be an emerging area, which might be a way for me to integrate all my skills and experience. It is too early to know. I still have not yet rediscovered my creative voices, such as writing poetry or doing pottery, but, very surprisingly, this new stage feels most like my twenties, when I was still trying to work out who I was, but then too quickly let myself be completely taken over by corporate and family life.

As I look back at this career story, what have I learnt? Firstly, that I am still writing my story. It took many different conversations and several drafts to create even this narrative of my career. I am sure that if I turned the kaleidoscope, I could come up with another set of patterns. I have started to understand better how my childhood development and family archetype have deeply influenced my sense of identity, my desire for safety or adventure and the way that I have approached my work life. I am still learning that work is not everything and does not need to embody all my "value"; I don't need to prove anything to myself (or the world) anymore, although that script remains compellingly strong.

I am also now fortunate enough to have two grown-up daughters with whom I am delighted to stay close, a strong marriage and many deep friendships – relationships to cherish; I remain passionately curious about many aspects of life and the world, and continue to love to discover and learn. I trust that I can create a tapestry of identities, if I want. And maybe, as my dear late friend prompted, over that spring lunch in Salisbury, just keep the stories rolling, for as long as I can. And the key lesson I am starting to draw from recasting my story, here, in my late stage work life, is to just try and enjoy what I am doing, at the moment, and show myself and others some compassion while doing so.

CHAPTER FOURTEEN

Building On Our Life Experience

A RESPONSE TO STEVEN FROM SUSIE

> Inside every old person is a young person wondering what happened.
>
> Terry Pratchett

Steven sensitively unwraps some of his life experiences and tries to make sense of the themes whilst also acknowledging the interesting shifts in his values and needs. He details, 'The scores on a number of my standard behavioural tests had changed from previous years. I no longer came out as so structured and task-driven, inflexible. Instead, scores around caring, intuition and creativity had risen significantly.'

Time passes and it can feel as though we are flipping through the decades of our lives. It seems entirely appropriate that the meaning of the noun 'career' is 'occupation through life', but what can seem more apt is the verb, defined as 'to move swiftly and in an uncontrolled way'!

The pieces in the book are written by clients exploring their life from the vantage point of a particular decade; the youngest writer is 29 and the oldest 63. Interestingly, though, the writers usually describe how it felt to be alive at a certain point in time rather than defining their life in terms of specific achievements and milestones. None of them see their age as the most significant characteristic. But something does seem to hit us when we approach a new decade. I'm often contacted by individuals on this threshold. Clients sense that this feels an appropriate time to look back but also explore the future.

Why is this? There seems to be a real need to reconceive and re-examine our lives to date and connect this with our future self as we age. Those big birthdays can feel like markers, times not only to celebrate but look back and wonder what is coming next. Rewind to my 40th birthday, spent in an exquisite Spanish hotel, its charms lying unnoticed by my tumultuous self . Life seemed to be passing too quickly. I was full of uncomfortable anxiety about the future. I was the mother of three young, dearly loved daughters but a bit lost. Searching for something else, something elusive and more profound?

This from the *Washington Post* (i): 'over the past decade or so, evidence has emerged from economics, psychology and neuroscience showing that humans tend to go through a kind of emotional reboot around midlife. It's often experienced as a period of malaise and dissatisfaction, but normally it is not — contrary to stereotype — a crisis. Rather, it is a transition. During this period, our values, our priorities, even our brains tend to shift away from competition and social striving and toward connecting and giving to others'. This emotional reboot can happen as early as 30, as Sean describes in chapter three, or as Cassie writes about in chapter nineteen. She beautifully describes what it feels like to come 'home' after leaving your place of birth, returning to live in the same geography but now carrying the wisdom of a few richly lived decades. She explains, 'Now I've chosen to come back to Birmingham and I'm reflecting on how the 25-year-old me would be furious with my choice. Why spend years trying to escape a place, only to return?'

Journey or destination?

Can understanding our life stages help us know what to expect and understand what others are experiencing in similar situations? The writers in this book transport us directly into the immediacy and the now of lived experience but can some of the ideas developed by psychologists, sociologists, philosophers and poets also enrich our understanding?

Donald Super (ii), an American psychologist, created his developmental self-concept theory in the 1950s, when the world was a very different place, and his proposition that we move from 'exploration', 'establishment', 'maintenance' and then 'decline' seems too fixed in 2023. It belies the fact that the average graduate will now have five different 'careers' in their lifetime. We are constantly reinventing ourselves. We have mini cycles in our working lives. Over the past few decades we have all had to become more intentional and entrepreneurial about how we manage our careers; the idea of a job for life has become both rare and less desirable. Instead of seeing ageing as a deficit model could we understand the process as one of growth? Accepting some of the physiological limitations we might have, but still looking for fulfilment? This is what the stories in this book seem to be telling us. And it happens all the time. Cassie, in chapter nineteen, now in her forties, explains: 'I do feel the need to explore what could be next, or new, and what I'll learn from the next instalment.'

Exploring his retirement as a partner of a large accountancy firm, my client, Kamal, explains the desire he had to develop a new 'career' in the arts: 'I have had to be prepared to push myself into the uncomfortable'. Kamal was now ready to shift his perspective: 'I am much more aware and sensitive to the significance of people who deliver things on a daily basis, who make things run.' And he examines this shift: 'my new work gives me exposure to a rich quality of ideas, thinking, the ability to discuss and debate.'

According to Danish psychologist Erik Erikson (iii), development occurs through a series of changes in the abilities of the ego, the rational component of our personality. Erikson proposed a set of stages, but he did not intend that the stages be understood as steps on a ladder. Instead, he maintained that people can grapple with any psychosocial issue at any time. However they are most likely to confront certain issues when they are in a particular age period. In your twenties, people begin to explore possibilities and form their own identity based upon the outcome of these explorations. Failure to establish a sense of identity within society (I don't know what I want to be when I grow up) can lead to role confusion. Role confusion involves the individual not being sure about themselves or their place in society. Erikson's term 'Generativity', often occurring in middle age, refers to a need to make your mark on the world through creating or nurturing something that will outlast the individual. It might also happen through creating positive change that benefits other people.

My client, Kate, reimagines the next stage of her life in her mid-forties: 'I feel an overriding need for change, to explore interests, film critiquing, casting, stand-up comedy, painting, singing, opening something in my community, studying therapy.' She has a powerful visual image of the future: 'I am working from the garden studio, the walls are full of images, drawings, words, the whole space is an aesthetic shrine to everything I love, hold dear and true and value. I am talking to 'clients' and peers on a daily basis, possibly travelling, but with a base at home. I have two "uniforms": one for the garden studio, massive red cardigans and elaborate earrings, and the other for "outside", tailored clothes with strong boots. Always comfortable knickers.'

Erikson believed that if we see our lives as unproductive, feel guilty about our past, or feel that we did not accomplish our life goals, we become dissatisfied with life and develop despair, often leading to depression and hopelessness. However if we can identify the success in each stage we cultivate something more like wisdom. Wisdom enables a person to look back on their life with a sense of closure and completeness, and also accept ageing without fear.

My client, Paul, imagines how he wants to be talked about when he is gone: 'In many ways his ambitions always outshone his capacity to achieve but achieve he did. And while these achievements were often the banishment of his fears, or the manifestation of his beliefs, they were always also the means by which he gave shelter and built space for his family and loved ones, who were his anchor and spur for much of his life and thought.'

'It was in those times, with them, that he was at peace, be it planting trees and observing their constant growth, or watching the stars with his grandchildren from the terrace of their country house, or cooking together, before sleeping in front of the log fire, books always to hand, his dogs at his feet.' Perhaps this is what is meant by wisdom?

Shifting to the new

The developmental psychologist Paul Baltes (iv) explores how specific cultures will hold certain expectations about how to live and work and how living in a given time and place will exert influence on an individual. I meet many people who decide to focus or shift their working lives towards addressing the challenges we face today; both societal and environmental. We live in a time of unprecedented challenge to the state of our planet. My client, Harriet, left her role in investment banking, studying for a Master's in environmental technology. She is now working as a researcher in a green bank focusing on ethical and sustainable investment.

I worked with Ahmet when he was finishing an executive Master's in management at the London School of Economics. After fifteen years as a consultant, he witnesses the challenges of human adaptation to artificial intelligence. He now fashions his work around AI and is hoping to study for a PhD on the subject. He explains: 'I have a fascination about how the human brain works. My extensive experience as a management consultant in organisational transformation and my passion to improve human life/conditions led me to focus on the development of strategies for AI implementation within organisations and taking part in leading these initiatives.'

Random unpredictable events that are idiosyncratic to that individual can act as a catalyst for a change in our career aspirations, sometimes helping us to appreciate the fragility of life and consider what we most value. My client, Julia, wonders about the randomness of her early career: 'I have been wondering lately what would have happened if I had pursued environmental journalism after college. That was after I'd applied to and been rejected from a few journalism internships – when I started pursuing other avenues and ended up accepting a job offer from the start-up I worked for. Just a couple of weeks later I got a call from one of my academic advisors saying that a contact of his at the *Washington Post* was looking for someone to shadow him. I'd already signed the contract with the start-up, so I passed on the offer, but I can't help but think my life would have turned out pretty differently had I taken the journalism job.'

REFLECT Some provocative questions for you to think about:

Ask yourself:

- What does the concept of career mean at this time of my life?
- Pick out the three or four things from your childhood that have had an impact on the person I am today. How are they reflected in my life and work? What am I grateful for from your past?
- What were major turning points in my life? Think about wise decisions, and other decisions. How did I react to these events? What lessons did I learn? Review anything that you consider a growth opportunity and the learning it afforded me.
- What new skills/ways of thinking have I picked up over time?
- What risks have I taken in my career? Where do I wish I'd taken more risk?
- If there was nothing holding me back, the things I would be trying out, doing or saying would be…
- What do I want more of in my life?
- What do I want less of in my life?
- What do I want to be remembered for at the end of my life?

Our coats of many colours

Robert Kegan (v), working in the 1980s, explored how each new iteration of the way that we see ourselves emerges when there are incongruities between how we see the world and new experiences; we then want to make sense of ourselves in a different way. Cassie explains how this works for her: 'I have taken some brave choices to move on into new roles and organisations, and to try on different versions of my own character identity to suit different stages of the plot, while I worked out what my own strengths (and flaws) and unique contribution can be.' I like the idea of an integrated self, drawing on sustenance of the past while still retaining a vital involvement in the present. This gives us the chance to see our life as a whole. We can come to terms with its meaning, purpose and shape instead of thinking of it as discrete stages.

Our life stages are connected, bleed into each other, and what happens in each affects all the stages to come. Our experiences build upon one another and prepare us for our future life.

Working with my clients, personal experience and research tells us that irrespective of life stages, its our ability to live fully in the moment that will enable us to flourish. That's your challenge for today!

CHAPTER FIFTEEN

Brighton Rock?

SERENA

I often wonder if there *is* such a thing as vocation. I felt from a young age that I was destined to be an actress. Was that nature, or nurture? Did I absorb the desire for acting through my mother's skin, through the look in my actor father's eye and from the blood of my actor grandfather? I used to say that if you cut me in half it would say *ACTRESS* all the way through, like a stick of Brighton Rock. Now I wonder whether that is true. Instead, it has occurred to me that, rather than finding a vocation, I just got caught up in an inherited system that I have always found difficult to leave.

As a small child, I wanted to be a nurse. I can remember the thrill of the nurse's outfit my parents bought for me; the blue cardboard case with special nurse's "things" in it, the joy of hitting my father's knee with the special hammer, and the endlessly entertaining kick of his leg. Perhaps the coup of actually having his undivided attention made this seem special, but I felt that I had found my place in the world; being kind and helping people to feel better.

Also, I *loved* human biology (as it was called in the 1970s); it was what un-sciencey girls did at my school instead of "ordinary" biology, whatever that was. It was the only un-arty subject that I really enjoyed.

Despite my keen interest, I perpetually felt like I was a weak student in my high-achieving girls' grammar school. Perhaps that was only my perception. I have often wondered whether my life could have taken a completely different turn, had I followed my urge to nurse, and then become a midwife (a work fantasy that I still frequently have). However, by the age of 12, it was too late; I had already been distracted by the magic of the theatre.

The inherent problem with being a third-generation actor, along with the obvious privilege that comes from being brought up as part of a family that understands, loves and is part of the theatrical circus, is that it chooses you, rather than the other way round. As a child, I became an honorary member of every theatre company that my father joined. For a child this was heaven, because actors are the best company you could ever wish for; they are inclined towards narcissism, so they *need* you to love them, and they are child-like, so they *want* to play.

Being an actor seemed like the most glamorous occupation compared to the jobs that my friends' parents did; they were all bank managers and doctors and teachers. It was the 1970s and there was an endless stream of actors in our home. They came, in flares and grandad vests, and sat around our kitchen table, drinking, laughing and flirting with each other. It was all or nothing, vocational, out of the norm, full of the promise and possibility of stardom. I fell for it, hook, line and sinker.

Now I wonder whether my decision to become an actor was also, in part, a way to be closer to my father. I adored him but, like most actors, he was consistently absent. Perhaps I felt, subconsciously, that the only way to capture him would be to follow him into the business?

I joined my village amateur dramatics group at 14 and loved not only expressing myself through acting, but also the joy of being part of my local community. I took part, with gusto, in plays, music hall evenings, and all types of village entertainments. In writing this now, I can see the connection with the theatres I so loved to work in as a professional actress: the Globe, Regent's Park, Scarborough, all closely connected to their communities.

At 17, in my A level year, I auditioned for Guildhall Drama School. Everyone knew that I was going to be an actress; surely it was a foregone conclusion that I would be offered a place?

I didn't get in. My A levels weren't good enough for further education, and now I hadn't got into drama school. Calamity!

A while later, a friend of my parents, who was on the auditioning panel at Guildhall, told them that they had felt that I didn't want to be there. I've often thought about that; what was the inner ambivalence that they could see? Now, with therapy and coaching under my belt, I can see that perhaps I had been heading down a slightly unsuitable route; even performing in my beloved village amateur dramatics had tapped into my need to be perfect, and to please. To be a successful actor, it helps to not care what others think of you. Even at 14, I wasn't confident in my looks or my body, and I found the inevitable scrutiny and judgment from audiences, directors, producers, hard to bear.

Nevertheless, I had a) told everyone that I was going to be an actress, and b), maybe even more powerfully, decided that I *wasn't* going to repeat my mother's pattern: to give up acting at the first hurdle. I ploughed relentlessly onwards.

That is not to say that I didn't love expressing myself through performance because I did (and still do). I have always loved the release and connection that finding my own personal path through a character brings. It is only in retrospect that I wonder if, at 17, I might have explored a few different avenues. Now, however, forty years later, I can see I was caught in the current of theatre and it was drawing me onwards.

So, in that summer after A levels, as my friends went to Greece on the Magic Bus, I headed to London, determined to earn my equity card in order to secure an acting job. My father was in a play in the West End, and he got me a job as a dresser, for a wonderfully kind and inspirational actress called Julia McKenzie. It was my job to collect her costumes, help her into them, polish her shoes, be available for changes during the show, fetch her cups of tea in the interval, and salt beef sandwiches (from the kiosk, long gone, on Windmill Street) on matinée days. If she had visitors, it was my job to make them Martinis, and hand round bowls of crisps. I loved it. I fell immediately in love with one of the assistant stage managers (gay, but that's how you learn). There was a tiny poisonous male dresser, who "looked after" Paul Eddington. He did not approve of me in any way. He always had a fag on the go, and he'd peer up at me through the rings of smoke, in my pink dungarees, pink hair and one earring, and say, 'What on earth is she wearing today?'

Despite his withering scorn, I still loved the job.

I used to travel into town with my father, and he would say, 'Give us a fag,' as we got on the train. This was forbidden at home, and now a secret between us. I was in the theatre, where 'nothing counts on tour'. That smoking habit would eventually kill him, of course, but that's a story for another day.

I found a second daytime job in a children's theatre, the Unicorn, working front of house, cooking in the cafe? and tearing tickets. I finished by 5pm so I could wander up through Chinatown, to my evening job. Eventually the Unicorn gave me a job in stage management, and then a tiny role in a kids' show. This was my first professional acting role and I earned my equity card. The stakes were low; no one was watching, or writing a review. I was doing it for the love of it.

I loved being part of two theatres, two communities. Some of the people I met then are still my friends today. Looking back, I think this was my happiest time in the theatre. I thrived on being part of a team; I felt needed, and I was helping a show to run smoothly. Every person in the theatre is a cog in the wheel; all are equally essential in creating the magic box. I was also, mostly, not performing;–the spotlight was not on me, so I felt no pressure.

However, acting continued to call to me, and four years on from my doomed Guildhall audition, I landed a place at Central School of Drama. I swear that no audition has ever been as scary or as satisfying as that one!

I loved drama school. Yet again, I thrived on being part of a collective and formed strong connections with my peers. Three years of working day after day with the same people and playing any number of wonderful parts was heaven. I knew my place and I loved it. I don't recall having any major performance anxiety at this time, only the usual adrenaline, nothing crippling or worrying. I loved learning my craft.

I went straight from Central into a year's contract of *Noises Off* at The Savoy theatre. For a first job, it was a coup, but by the end of the fourth month I was maddened by the repetition, and I still had another eight months to go. It was the first inkling that theatre was not all it was cracked up to be. Performance anxiety also began to rear its ugly head. I found that the endless repetition of the same words night after night began to exhaust me, and at some point, I remember making my mother ring the company manager to wangle me a night off. I found that relentless year very hard.

In theatrical circles it feels almost forbidden to declare that you no longer want to be an actor. You're told that it is the *only* thing that anyone could wish to do with their lives – 'Darling! It's *such* fun!' – and, if you are lucky enough to make a living at it, then you should never question its place in your life. We are all there on a wing and a prayer, and it has always felt that I was supposed to be supremely grateful that the theatre gods had deigned to find me employment. In fact, I had worked incredibly hard to be successful; I *earned* my place in the theatre. Nonetheless, even writing this now, feels wicked and ungrateful. To consider leaving acting still feels almost sacrilegious; the commitment is complete and for life.

Despite my misgivings during *Noises Off*, it didn't occur to me to stop acting. I had a plan, which was to be a highly successful comic actress, and the pull of that vision led me onwards.

Even before I went to drama school I had set my heart on working for Alan Ayckbourn, who was running his own theatre in Scarborough. In the 1970s and '80s Ayckbourn was *the* person who was writing wonderful parts for women; funny, decent-sized parts, which was unusual then. The dream was to work for him in Scarborough, have a part written for me, play it in the summer season, and then transfer with it to the West End the following year. This was what I had set my heart on and, amazingly, after my year in *Noises Off*, it unfolded exactly as I had planned. I was given a wonderful run of parts for the summer season and I returned the following year to play a role, written for me, in a brand new play. Working for Alan Ayckbourn, in Scarborough, was a dream. I was working in a small town, in an intimate theatre, creating new pieces of work. In this context, I felt no performance anxiety; I was laughing, singing, feeling the joy of being a part of a company. At the same time, I met my soon-to-be husband. All was perfect.

So what did I do? I added a baby into the mix. I returned to

Scarborough to play the most exciting part of my life, written especially for me, pregnant.

Everything collided around the uncomfortable combination of success and babies, just as it had with my mother. The difference being that I stubbornly, desperately wanted both. Looking back now on the 27-year-old me, I truly thought I could have it all (as *Cosmopolitan* had told us we could).

I managed to get through the play before I got too enormous, but I had such horrible morning sickness that the smell of my leading man's aftershave was unbearable. In one scene I had to prance about in my undies (it *was* the '80s) and the knickers had to have more and more elastic added to the waistline as time wore on. However I was a success in this play; it was my dream part, and the producer wanted me to do it in the West End. They were also prepared to wait for me to have the baby. All of this was amazing, thrilling, magical, exciting. I knew I was good, I knew that this sort of part didn't come around very often, if at all, and I knew I had to make the absolute most of it. That meant getting childcare sorted, and heading back into the theatre every night for nine months, leaving my tiny baby at home.

A year later, I played the part, opposite Ian McKellen, in the West End. I was nominated for an Olivier Award in the 1988 SWET awards. It was everything an aspiring actress could possibly want. But, but, but … I HAD A BABY. I was exhausted. I had so little energy. Again, I was bored after the first couple of months of repetition night after night. I learnt transcendental meditation in the hope that it would sort me out, I drank special '80s-style guarana drinks to whizz me up before I went on stage, but something was broken. My desire for it, my drive, the romance were all gone and I was just plain worn out.

Truthfully, as an actress, I have never recovered from this time. I had created the dream, and it had all happened as I planned it. However, putting a baby into the mix had put a spanner in the works. I can see now that there were the seeds of a richer life in this apparent failure to thrive; was it pointing me towards needing a different kind of life? The theatre felt so "all or nothing" that I couldn't see my way past the black and white notions of success or failure. My family history was all about "being a star", so to be anything less than that seemed like failing.

Now I wonder if perhaps I needed more support? Probably, but I didn't know that I did, and I certainly didn't know how to ask. Or perhaps I had simply achieved what I had set out to do, and it was the end of that particular road. Either way I began to withdraw; we moved out of London, I turned down a six-month extension on my contract and I then turned down a brilliant part in another funny play in the West End. All of this seemed rational to me, but not to producers, agents, parents, or my husband. Even now feel that I let myself down; it's a painful memory, but I just couldn't keep it up.

I think that the seeds of performance anxiety must have taken root in this year; my exhausted body and my exhausted spirit were sending me very clear messages. Stop! Do Not proceed! Take a break! I can see that I didn't have the constitution or the push to keep motoring forwards towards 'stardom', to play the game, to schmooze the casting agents. Now I understand myself, and can offer compassion to the exhausted Serena, but I didn't back then. As far as I was concerned, I had blown the star-spangled career that I had been aiming towards. Babies and West End theatre don't mix, or at least, not for me.

I'm making it sound as though that was the end of my career, which it most certainly wasn't. It's important to say that I loved (and still love) the skill and the thrill of comedy. I love to fill the boots of a character, whoever she is, and I love to express parts of myself that don't get an airing in everyday life. It is the physical and mental exhaustion that I found (and still find) difficult.

For the next thirty years, I continued to work in the West End, did television comedy, toured around all the theatres in the country, worked with the National Theatre and travelled the world with the Royal Shakespeare Company. I worked for wonderful companies such as Regent's Park Open Air theatre and Shakespeare's Globe.

It is always heaven to be part of a company of actors who laugh together, work hard together, create something beautiful together and then thrill an audience together. When this special mix happens in a theatre company, it feels like you are the luckiest person alive.

I eventually I found my correct place in the theatre. I know that I am not a leader; I am not made to be a "star£. Instead, I take pleasure in being part of the team. I pride myself on being a "foot soldier". It takes immense fortitude to be a star; it also takes drive and ego, stubbornness, and strength. I have all of those qualities, but I also wanted babies and family and a life outside the theatre. I eventually found my comfortable place as a performer, always in work, using my talent to tell stories and entertain. This still gives me great pleasure.

However my acting career did not touch the part of me that loves helping others. As time went on, I felt increasingly interested in how people work and began to move towards a more nourishing working life for myself. At 42, I met and trained as a coach with Nancy Kline (@Time to Think). Nancy taught me to listen to others with care and respect, and to understand that we all hold our own answers if we are given the space. With Nancy, I had my first experience of being listened to without interruption, and I learnt to offer that simple discipline to others in a group or coaching context. At the same time, I also became very interested in Lee Glickstein's work (Speaking Circles) which is about standing up in front of others and speaking from your heart, in the moment. After years of learning and expressing others' words and thoughts, this pure access to my own thinking was a revelation. I can now see that I longed to be heard, and began to long to offer this to others. To me, the voice and the stories that emerge when we are given space is equally as rich and creative as any piece of theatre. This has been a constant in my life since then. I love to encourage and hear people's stories. I want to create and hold the space for others to express themselves, so that they can find their place in the world.

A foundation in psychotherapy followed, and a year studying Systemic Constellations, a therapeutic approach that looks at the hidden dynamics within the systems in which we live, at work, in families, in relationships. This was followed by a year studying Voice for Actors, with Patsy Rodenberg at Guildhall School. I was clearly hungry for new paths.

What I noticed, however, was that, whenever I came vaguely close to committing to a new start, or career, an acting job would pop up, and I'd take myself back into the theatre fold. Of course, it was my safe space, and I loved it, *and* hated it, all at the same time. Importantly, it represented money and stability. Having lived my whole life with actors, I was grounded in never ever turning work down, because you never know where your next pay cheque is coming from. Perhaps, also, there were elements of FOMO: 'If I say no, then it will be the end of me.'

In 2012, my husband and I left London and moved to Pembrokeshire, something we had thought about and planned for years. At the age when acting work for women becomes almost non-existent, the physical distance allowed me to start to rethink how I work.

Whilst still being open to acting turning up (and it does), I now run courses and workshops for people to find their voice. I love this work. I am always thrilled and moved to witness participants flourish and shift in front of my eyes. My forty years of work in theatre, and all the training I have done over the years, plays a huge part in this. The work centres on an encouragement to be yourself, to understand that we are communicating creatures who tell stories to teach, or to be understood, and that we do it naturally. Somehow, we have forgotten this innate talent that we all share. Perhaps the fear of revealing ourselves and our vulnerabilities holds us back. Indeed, time and time again, I have witnessed participants, who have a fear of speaking out, find their voice, and go on to inspire, move and thrill others with their stories.

Is this my vocation? To help others to feel better about standing up and expressing themselves? I am still not sure that there is such a thing; instead there seems to be a constant stream of choices to be made. This last pandemic year I have not only trained to be a coach, but I also received coaching from Susie. Her strong, kind approach has helped me to look back at my career with compassion, and to notice what I do well, where my skills are, and to understand what I actually enjoy. I have also learnt that I have resilience and staying power, which has been astonishing for me to realise.

The reframing that has come through Susie's coaching has

completely shifted the way I see myself and my career. In this strange pandemic year, I have missed being part of a team; I am not at my best working by myself. However, I now love the fact that I can work online, running courses and seeing clients, when so many actors have been left high and dry by the situation. Living and working in the wilds of Pembrokeshire is a rich and continuing adventure.

I had an internalised vision that I think I created at a very young age – it was of a shining star, nothing less, who was not only brilliant, and loved by all, but also happy. The vision was so singular that I couldn't allow myself any wiggle room so when it faltered, I thought I'd failed. Anything, whatever it was, that came after seemed like a pale imitation of success.

What advice would the 61-year-old Serena give to her younger self, who spent so many years thinking that she was hopeless? Well, looking back I am amazed and moved by the courage, adaptability, energy, optimism, skill and sustainability that the young Serena showed. I would love retrospectively to give the 18-year-old Serena the gift of confidence; the confidence to listen to her own heart, and to follow her own drum down some unforeseen dark alleys. Above all, I would give her the confidence to realise that when you allow the story of your life to unfold in ways that you cannot control or foresee, that is when the magic happens; and that the magic is *never* what you expected in the first place.

CHAPTER SIXTEEN

Career Tensions

A RESPONSE TO SERENA FROM SUSIE

> There's a constant tension in climbing, and really all exploration, between pushing yourself into the unknown, but trying not to push too far. The best any of us can do is to tread that line carefully.
>
> Alex Honnold

Wouldn't it be great if you could feed all our personal data into a computer and, hey presto, your dream career pops up! No more agonising around work dilemmas or career choices. Serena's story illustrates how are our choices are so nuanced and complex. As an actor she was sometimes bored, sometimes terrified, frequently anxious, often admired and sometimes exhilarated. Those deeply felt tensions eventually drove her to consider another way of life.

As we will have read in the client stories, there is often a trade-off between following a passion or another more stable and secure choice. We could decide that our need for autonomy and independence will be best suited with freelance work, but this now means we won't be leading a team. We might feel fearful of initiating the new when we can stick to the tried and tested. The tensions we experience between perhaps loving the unpredictability of interacting spontaneously with people and working with new issues versus wanting to get things right and plan so nothing goes awry. One of my clients explores this: 'I am highly imaginative and openminded. I thrive in environments which value experimentation, innovation and progress. However, I'm also cautious and like to have strong foundations before making a decision.' Or maybe later in life, as we transition from a high status corporate role, we miss the power that the role gave us to make things happen. However we also want to learn by doing something more community orientated. Steven explores this in his story in chapter thirteen. One part of ourselves is drawn in one direction and another part in something which appears apparently contradictory.

The trade-off

This tension demands that we make some sort of decision. It would be lovely to find a role that met all our values simultaneously, but that's pretty difficult. If such an option existed, a decision would be unnecessary. Whatever we decide, there are bound to be winners and losers and it's this tension between what to act upon and what to leave behind that feels challenging. However, the dilemmas we experience allow us to dig deeper and explore our priorities. If we can resolve the conflict and tension, it will really help us to have more agency in shaping our working life.

We all have these dynamic tensions which arise because of our personalities, the messages we received growing up or the visions and values we hold dear. The problem with allowing this mythical computer to make the choices for us is that life isn't always rational; we often make decisions based on something more instinctive or emotional. Psychologists often use the term mental model or cognitive map to describe the inner road map we use. This helps us both consciously and unconsciously to make decisions of all types and sizes. We now know more about how the brain works and know that our rational pre-frontal cortex is partnered with a more 'emotional brain' that processes a huge amount of information beneath this conscious level. We sometimes make up our minds before we know it ourselves. My client writes, 'I like to have space to think strategically and consider the bigger picture and context I'm operating within.' The issues with a mental model, such as the previous statement, is that it operates on information from the past. Its pretty tough to take in all that 'in the past' information, stand back from it and incorporate new ideas and new tests.

So how can we test our thoughts and plans against the best

available evidence we have right now? I was working with a client who was giving a presentation to a team of newly hired senior executives. Something felt wrong for him. A sense of unease and disquiet with the behaviour in the team. What was this about? For my client, Rishi, it was a sense that his deeply held values around how you treat others was being challenged. But Rishi loves his role; can he work with the new people who have different ways of behaving and treating others? The tensions were beginning to emerge. We had explored a new style of leadership which was both curious and compassionate. He wanted to build the confidence to champion his newfound leadership style to shift the culture but also feel some of the tensions that he was experiencing dissipate.

Working along the continuum

We may find as a leader at work that we experience a tension between supporting and nurturing others and our own need to control and shape the agenda. My client, Ali, felt that these tensions were stopping her being a strong leader. She began to reflect more on the instinctive behaviour and emotions that didn't serve her and then started to learn from and change these patterns. This was especially around her need for control. Ali began to set her intentions for reflection on how she would show up each day and this stopped her consistently being caught up in solving the day-to-day or other people's needs. Taking the time to think about her unique skills, where she got her energy from and what she brought to the team helped her to resolve some of the tension and reignited her aspirations and ambition. This led to some powerful feedback: 'Ali is an extremely effective communicator and is capable of tailoring her style accordingly in any setting. She inspires the team by balancing her role as an advisor with that of a coach, listening intently and empowering individuals (and groups) to find their way through to their own solutions. Her leadership style, which feels as though it has evolved from 'pace-setting' to 'coaching' over the last year, is highly appreciated across the team and her input and involvement inspires the team to higher performance.'

Sometimes your tensions can be resolved by exploring the broader themes or interests that give your work meaning. Take a look at this table of Ten Basic Interests. Which of these areas resonate with you? Are there any tensions between the interests?

TEN BASIC INTERESTS

Most of us have significant interests in more than one of the ten dimensions; some of us even have significant interest in four or more. Which of these interests has resonance for you?

The Engineer: APPLICATION OF TECHNOLOGY – innovation, problem solving, planning, engineering, science, gadgets, cutting edge technology

The Number Cruncher: QUANTITATIVE ANALYSIS – finance, analysis, control, maths, forecasting, modelling, precision

The Professor: THEORY DEVELOPMENT AND CONCEPTUAL THINKING – learning, problem solving, teaching, research, ideas, debate, imagination, theory

The Artist: CREATIVE PRODUCTION – brainstorming, creating new projects, fast pace, free thinking, loving ideas

The Coach: COUNSELLING AND MENTORING – relationships, altruism, social enterprise, teaching, counselling, psychology

The Team Leader: MANAGING PEOPLE AND RELATIONSHIPS – teams, leader, manager, mentor, goals, vision, motivation

The Boss: ENTERPRISE CONTROL – strategy, vision, leadership, control, ownership, power, decision maker, player

The Persuader: INFLUENCE THROUGH LANGUAGE AND IDEAS – ideas, knowledge, persuasion, writing, speeches,communication, power of language, influence, presentation

The Action Hero: HANDS ON PROBLEM SOLVING – action, service ,craft, skill, strength, sports, tangible results, tools

The Organizer: ORDERING INFORMATION – order, routine, predictability

REFLECT

How can you begin to explore and resolve these tensions for yourself?

1. Go deep into your options
2. Look at life more broadly
3. Is this value transitory or deeper?
4. Refine and reconceptualise
5. What might you need to develop?
6. Which are complimenting values?
7. Which values should prevail?

Let's look at these solutions one by one. Sometimes our judgements might be too extreme or actually not even correct. Chris was working for a financial regulation agency and assumed she might not be able to use her conceptual and creative thinking. As she has developed her 'craft' she has become known for her ability to innovate and take responsibility for creative projects. Try not to assess a role too superficially. Ask yourself what are the possibilities for growth? How might they allow me to use my strengths and what is important to me? Roles really do change over time.

Pasqual was relishing his role as a brand strategist; he was a real expert and loved the intellectual challenge in his job. And yet there was a tension between this and his need for nurturing others, especially those less advantaged. He secured a voluntary role mentoring inner city boys and found that this role gave him the extra satisfaction he was missing in his full-time position.

Finding what's enduring

Sometimes our values can be somewhat transitory: a peer group we find ourselves in, a romantic relationship, a travel experience. Can we trace the basis for this value and try to understand whether it will be something more enduring or more momentary?

We might find that we really need to dig deeper to refine, extend or elaborate the tension that we are feeling. Can you conceive your value of say, influencing through language and ideas (see Ten Basic Interests above) to shape your role differently? Take responsibility for writing new thought pieces? Presenting your work across the business? Can you redefine what success looks like in the role? Or refine your role? My client, Phil, did this and writes: 'I was missing a sense of connection with others in my role. I have been building depth in my relationships with those who influence my career progression. This has led to the opportunity to have further conversations which are less transactional and feel more personal and meaningful.'

Chris recounts her experiences: 'I also initially attempted to work four days a week (for 80% pay) but found myself working 60+ hours a week and hating it.' The familiar tension between work and personal life can mean you take more control of the boundaries as you resolve these tensions.

We might find two values might be at odds. However, if we think of what makes a good life, incompatible values can sometimes, on reflection, feel complementary. For example, income and time off might conflict with one another, but each might be important in maintaining the quality of family life. By seeing how each value complements the other as a means toward a common end, a conflict is placed in perspective.

Perhaps the easiest way to resolve tension is to determine which value is most important. We don't necessarily need to decide between options but between values. Explore the relative advantages and disadvantages for the future. Chris did some journalling about the three or four pillars of what was most important to her. She told me, 'I wrote about things I want to be present in my role and then started to share these points with others. It was very challenging but invaluable and has given me a framework for decisions since and helped me feel confident talking about my story and with more confidence and clarity.'

The tensions in your career will always be present, but shedding light on what these are and exploring them more deeply will give you a stronger sense of control in the decisions that we make and the path that we follow.

CHAPTER SEVENTEEN

The Biggest 'F' In the Room

DIANA

It is the first week of my executive MBA. I am in the room with my new classmates. We are sitting in a circle. I am expectant, excited, somewhat fearful. I am sizing everyone up, trying to divine who will be the straight A student, who will just cruise by. Who will be my friend, who will be a stranger, who might dislike me? I wonder why, long past my school days, I still need so fiercely to belong.

In the leadership course, we are being placed into small groups. We will get to know each other, collaborate, disagree, be coached and challenged. We are discussing the results of our Myers-Briggs test, what those shiny little letters mean, for our colleagues, our study mates, our work lives.

The Myers-Briggs is a personality assessment, designed to enable an individual to understand how they perceive the world and then process this information. It comprises a series of questions to identify personality on the basis of four basic preferences or continuums: Extraversion (E)/Introversion (I), Sensing (S)/Intuition (N), Thinking (T)/Feeling (F), Judging (J)/Perceiving (P).(i) It is not the first time I've taken it. I like the safety of scales, grades, words on a page to tell me who I am and where I am going. I was always proud of my 'intuitive' score, my ability to piece up the world into a complex tapestry, to see, beyond loose threads and tight knots, a picture emerging. Today, it is the F that is glaring at me from the page, hooking me in with a scatter of question marks.

I am the biggest F in the room, that's what they are telling me. I am F, in a sea of Ts.

An F person makes decisions based on how those decions might affect other people involved. They feel unsettled by conflict. They are guided by their heart and find objectivity a challenge. 'Feelers' can be perceived as 'touchy-feely', overly idealistic and indirect.

What does 'driven by feeling' mean to me? How has it shaped my choices, the way I enter a room, earn a living, go to sleep or lay awake at night? How I replay the day's interactions in my head and process all that's raging on inside me? F is a super power, like an apprentice witch, that I am still trying to master. Feeling for me is a strength and a deep burrow. It is blazing and hiding, enthusiasm and burnout. F has a lot to do with why I am in this room full of curiosity and energy. But I am also back in school to tame the boredom, the disappointment, the blind rage of dead ends.

Professionally, I am conscientious, reliable, addicted to praise, cripplingly perfectionist. Prone to enthusiasm and despair. Energetic and impulsive. Problem solver, conflict avoidant. Longing for meaningful connection with others and with myself. Growing in work has meant a journey of self-discovery and self-mastery. It has been a process of understanding my strengths and challenges as an F, developing emotional agility and resilience, finding and asserting boundaries.

Thinking back, I guess I've been an F since day one. A sensitive child, an unbearably righteous teenager. Loved, sheltered, raised in sunny, ancient beautiful places, I had the privilege of being shocked by suffering.

This keen interest in the world and a hyper-awareness of its contrasts came from listening to my parents and their friends reminisce about working in Africa in the 1970s. Inevitably, at the dinner table, a few glasses of wine in, the stories would flow. Memories of remote and exotic places and different and friendly people captured my imagination. Growing up in Italy, I was surrounded by timeless beauty, natural and human-made. A keen student, I loved reading and learning. I discovered that humans are capable of creativity, ingenuity, courage and kindness. As a species, we are meaning making, storytelling, we make art that outlasts us. Yet I also learned that the world wasn't all heroic humans and happy endings.

My parents' tales explored the aftermath of the Nigerian civil war, the famine in Ethiopia, kidnappings and coups, the ambivalence of white privilege. Closer to home, my city was gripped by a heroin epidemic, young people wasted at street corners, and fear of AIDS. My Catholic school taught me empathy and compassion with a substantial side of shame and guilt. As a teenager I was studious, serious, sensitive and dramatic. Possibly a strange mix of rebellious and people-pleasing, both over-confident and scared of judgment. I was passionate and independent yet also self-involved and self-conscious. An avid reader of philosophy, politics and journalism, I looked for a way to make sense of these complicated feelings about the world. I hoped to resolve the contrast between the joy and lightness of my childhood and the darkness and deprivation so much of the news exuded.

Successfully academic, motivated and energetic, I felt a career to 'make it right' would be a good place to start. As I was about to leave school I was torn between *otium* and *negotium*, two Latin words that indicate the struggle between wanting a life of contemplation, holed up in my books and immersed in my beautiful and privileged surroundings, or a life of action, a life of purpose, a life for others. At that particular fork, it was action that won. I wanted to save the world, run the UN, right all the wrongs, stop the wars. Politics, journalism, history, humanism, I took it all in with incredible hubris. Everything was going to be okay, I was going to fix it. I'd get a job that would fix it.

I chose a career propelled by my emotional response to the world around me. I studied politics, then international relations, then development, with particular focus on gender equality and the rights of women internationally. I worked in the non-profit sector, government, multilateral diplomacy.

Curiosity lead me to travel, from the Hindu Kush to the source of the Nile, through war zones, budding democracies, corridors of power, heart-breaking slums. A deep sense of justice has given me purpose, but also the numbing fatigue of being a drop in the ocean. A longing for belonging and mentorship meant I always had high expectations of organisations and bosses, and felt crushing disappointment when, inevitably, these fell short of the pedestal.

The sketches that follow are moments of discovery that have shaped me as an individual and a leader. They were moments of change, moments where ideas and feelings collided with reality, teaching me that the world is not black and white but a kaleidoscope of iridescent colours.

This first story is about war.

I am sleepy yet alert, in the time-warp, in-between world of international airports. I'll get accustomed to the strangeness of this passage, between my world and the unknown. Stepping off into the night, the sudden slap of heat, dusty roads and new trees will become familiar features of my job, but I don't know that yet. This is my first time. My first time en route to a developing country, my first time en route to a war zone. I am about to learn about contrast, about rabbit holes, about liminal spaces.

My first taste of this twilight is Terminal 2, Dubai International Airport. I just spent six hours in Terminal 1, startled by rows of 24-carat gold, brightly coloured Lamborghinis. I am high from the pungent unctuosity of expensive fragrance, dusky jasmine, frankincense and rose. Terminal 2 is a few minutes from Terminal 1, but worlds away. It is empty, humid, austere. The departures board is sparce, two old UN humanitarian air services, rescued from the scrapyard, waiting on the runway, one to Baghdad, mine to Kabul. I wait to board and, as the sun is rising, a wave of arms ripple gently to the floor, in unison, whispering the morning prayer.

My first sight of this new country is the plane winding its descent between stunning mountain ranges, capped with snow, crumbling like brown sugar. The dust is everywhere, on the runway packed with military planes, in the streets. The city bears the scars of old wars but teems with life, carts full of oranges, battered taxis overflowing with passengers, bicycles, donkeys, military convoys, music. And people, men hunched on their heels, watchful, children playing, joyful, women standing, shrouded in clouds of cornflower blue. I lived and worked in a hotel in the eastern part of town at the foot of the mountain. Everyone coveted the rooms on the mountain side, safer from the mortars; I was told to sleep next to a packed emergency bag, ready to run. I worked late in the night in the top-floor, glassed-windowed office, the winter wind hurling outside. (Years later, back in London, I would wake one morning to the news that this hotel had been stormed, staff and guests held hostage. On television, I would watch the top floor burn, my former office up in flames against the dusty sky.)

I had prepared for this journey. I had read a lot about this country and thought I had the tools to make sense of it, understand the problems it faced. I would connect with the people there. My job was to conduct primary research on the security and humanitarian situation in the southern part of the country, interview people, document facts and publish a report to draw the world's attention to a Western intervention that was essentially failing. I thought that as a western person, with education, resources and goodwill, I could be part of the solution. There was part of me that felt elated, that congratulated myself for my "bravery", that felt a rush of excitement. I was naïve. I wasn't prepared for the fear, for the bewilderment, the pain, the anger, for the shame I felt. I wasn't prepared to understand that the people I met, the people I worked with, the people I was there to serve, weren't cast in the heroic tragedy I was playing out in my own head. They were real people, tri-dimensional, with real pain and real bravery, real flaws and real challenges. I met women who received death threats because they continued to teach girls to read and write. They did it anyway, even as their fellow teachers were decapitated. I met farmers whose harvest was destroyed by the conflict, communities with a violent distrust of strangers.

I got to know my own local colleagues, and the different risks that they faced. Those who were arrested when our office was stormed and our laptops confiscated while my shiny foreign passport could get me out of trouble and the country anytime. I got to know the contradictory world of expats and humanitarians. Kind, committed people, people with immense dedication, but also lost, damaged people, addicted to the adrenaline, a life on the edge. Beautiful Afghan music concerts at the French consulate, where I only gained acceptance because of my stint at a 'prestigious' university in Paris. The bars, the parties, the booze, the sorrow in the eyes of trafficked women, collateral damage to a place with too many soldiers. I saw locally co-led and co-created initiatives achieve respite and rebuilding, but also saw waste and fragmentation in project delivery. I witnessed intense competition for funding and the disastrousness of good intentions: food distribution networks crippling local bakeries, deserted schools built on donor assumptions rather than local need, the first mile of road disintegrating before the final was laid.

This "feeling overdose", the combination of purpose and helplessness, the line between constructive action and misguided time-wasting took several years to percolate into my leadership style. Ultimately it helped me design and deliver international initaitives more thoughtfully. It helped me understand that good intentions are a necessary but not sufficient motivation for in-country interventions. It underscored the importance of interrogating and redrawing re-evaluating my assumptions. The primacy of local need and local ownership stood out to me and the problematic nature of external solutions.

Working with people from backgrounds, cultures and experiences so utterly different from mine has been challenging but also freeing. One of the most challenging parts of being an F has been the intensity of my own feelings. A coping strategy has been chronic 'people pleasing'. I read a definition recently that really resonated with me: 'In reality it's a desire to organise the reactions of other people and avoid the discomfort their dislike brings up in you. People-pleasing is a strategy designed to keep you safely in control, wrapped up in a veneer of pseudo-generosity or flexibility.'(ii) Working with people from different cultures meant I could not easily read the reactions of others and I had to learn to become more authentic.

These lessons didn't manifest themselves immediately, but after many years of reflection, through individual psychotherapy and Susie's career coaching. At the time I didn't really have the ability to manage these feelings. I continued to travel widely, working on health projects in conflict environments, urban slums, prisons. I couldn't hold my tears in, standing in a landslide in Manila's port slums, as an eight-year-old orphan told me sniffing glue was a better investment than food, as it staved off his hunger for a whole week. I was gently reprimanded by my local counterpart: 'Please don't cry, you'll shame him.' The long hours, the travel, the pain and the helplessness took their toll. The breakdown of a long-term relationship, under-investment in friendships, a quarter-life crisis, crippling panic attacks. I burned out. I quit the job, spent the summer in Italy, sheltered by bewildered yet ever supportive parents.I was lulled by the quiet routine of a beach town; sleep, eat, swim, repeat. A few months of solo travel, the burnished gold of New York's avenues, bags of boiled crabs in Washington's harbour, the icy breeze off lake Ontario, afternoons curled up in the majestic corners of American public libraries. The luxury of self-care, of aimlessness.

With Susie, we worked to find a way back to a more authentic and resilient self. I had yet to understand 'feelings as data not directive'. Back in London, I needed anchoring. I took a job in a government agency, where I'd work to leverage international processes to advance domestic policy agendas. Working closer to home responded to a number of my needs and feelings. I felt less of an impostor, trying to "fix" things at home rather than abroad, where everything felt too complex and chaotic. Brussels and Geneva also felt an easier distance to negotiate, allowing for more work-life balance, more time to invest in steady friendships, in less chaotic romantic relationships. However, my ambitions were still somewhat grandiose and I felt incredibly passionate about my work.

My second story is about lobbying.

The countryside runs fast beyond the glass window, mist clinging to the sleepy fields. I look at my watch, running late. I mentally calculate the time it'll take me to negotiate the chaos of the station to emerge in the grey jungle of Brussels bureaucracy. I check my diary, packed. I open my files, reread the research, test my arguments, practice persuasion. I am giving evidence to a parliamentary committee voting on strengthening protection for pregnant workers. I am meeting with the European Commission on proposals to advance representation on corporate boards. I am holding the pen for a new strategy to end violence against women and girls in Europe. I care deeply about each of these issues. I have thoroughly enjoyed working with the policy experts. I can understand the research behind proposals, the pros and the cons, what is tried and tested, what we are experimenting with, how we calculate the financing, the impact on people's lives. I have loved identifying the most effective processes, the mapping stakeholders. I was riveted by planning tactics. Rubbing of shoulders in corridors behind parliamentary chambers, sparring with sceptics at cocktail parties and horse-trading with words. I pushed against BATNAs (the Best Alternative To a Negotiated Agreement), charm offencing those who could bring it over the line. Lots of people find policy work boring at best, ruthless at worst. I loved it. To me it was intellectually stimulating, purposeful. I found the competiveness of it compelling, winning arguments gave me a rush. I found a crowd of likeminded people, a bunch of creative bureaucrats who quietly and determinedly were changing the world.

Policy work enriched me but also brought out some more of my F shortcomings. An excess of idealism made me underestimate the timeframe needed for radical policy change. After months of chiselling at a file, moving it only three words forward, my enthusiasm waned. The snakes and ladders of political approvals meant a successful parliamentary vote could still be wrangled down by an unsympathetic Council. Compromise watered down months of hard graft. Personal agendas derailed projects, changes in government led us straight back to square one. "Computer says no" and the risk averseness of large bureaucratic machines alienated me. I struggled with boundaries, mistaking like-mindedness for infatuation and embarking on a disastrous romantic relationship with a counterpart. Austerity started to bite, colleagues on more insecure contracts packed their desks and funding for progressive social policy dried up. The financial crisis of the late naughties set in motion a cycle of events: austerity, populism, Brexit, which unravelled the certainty that we were riding an inevitable wave of equality and progress. I became restless. Moving on to the next job seemed easier than making sense of the ambivalence of my current experience.

The problem with feelings is that you can't really run from them, and in my new beginnings I was doomed to get tripped up by the same old hurdles. In the new job I had my own office, an executive assistant and a substantially larger salary. I had the mandate to support governments across the world establish effective institutions, reform policies, share good practice. Again, a lot to get characteristically F enthusiastic about, yet plenty of F sabotage opportunities. I brought to this job the learning from the previous years, a resized sense of self and better grasp on my own ability and the scope of my impact. I was more prepared, more patient and more resilient. Nevertheless, in this role I hit another major F faultline: bosses.

So much of my workplace relationships were shaped by my early experiences. Growing up I had an interesting relationship with authority figures. My parents have always been supportive and extremely loving, but at times could be strict and demanding. They are both, in their own way, quite emotional people, and I've always thought of their relationship as a tropical summer: warm and glowing, with sudden breaks of thunder.

Looking back now, as an adult who struggles with her own feelings, I can see how they also struggled with boundaries. I think my mother in particular couldn't bear for my sister and me to ever suffer, and was intensely and intrusively anxious. As a sensitive child, I found the intensity of my environment both familiar and intimidating. As the other members of my family were comfortable wearing a gamut of emotions on their sleeve, slipping in and out of them with ease, my feelings felt like hot treacle: messy and lingering. I had trouble recognising what feelings belonged to me and which ones to others. I felt like a sponge, soaking up and lugging aroud this heavy, uncomfortable weight. I managed to embrace positive feelings but repressed negative ones, particularly anger. My body became an "armour" to hold back a thundering wave of feeling. I strained in a near constant state of alertness, developing an unattainable need for safety and acceptance. As I grew up, while adventure was a hallmark of the work I sought, timidity was the watchword for engaging with people within it. I had trouble verbalising negative emotions in the workplace, avoiding confrontation, not asserting myself and my boundaries. When the

151

bottled-up feelings became too much, I just got another job and left.

At school, I adored my teachers and basked in their glowing praise. I was hardworking and dedicated, yet I eschewed the subjects I wasn't naturally talented at, and rebelled against those who gave me developmental feedback. I was unable to develop a 'growth mindset' because the feeling associated with growth, uncertainty and failure, just didn't feel safe to me. I came to believe that if the outcome was perfect, I wouldn't need to "feel" the bad stuff. If I was perfect, I would always feel included and loved.

In work, I have always been a perfectionist. I enjoyed anticipating and exceeding expecations. In the teams I managed, I aimed to create the nurturing and accepting environments I craved. I had high expectations of myself, my team and my bosses. My managing up and managing down style was very much shaped by the 'relational dowry', the imprints and baggage, of my upbringing.

So this last story is about office politics.

New job, new office, different challenges. The main challenge was my boss. I think some of the clues had been there at interview, but I was so ready to move from my previous job that I ignored them. A very high turnover in the team I was joining should have rung alarm bells. The rumours circulating about the person I would work for should have alerted me, but I didn't have the confidence to ask the right questions. I brushed off the temporary nature of the contract, not understanding that it would place me in a position of vulnerability. Over a period of five years, this person made my life very difficult. However this adverse experience enabled me to question and reset my problematic pattern of work relationships.

The constantly shifting priorities meant I couldn't readily meet and exceed expectations. I had to learn what "good enough" was for me. I had to find motivation independently from others' praise. For my own wellbeing, I had set some really strong boundaries against unpredictable behaviour. I learned to turn the phone off overnight, disconnecting from the stress of last-minute requests and early morning panicked calls. I learned to push back against the expectation that I would be available for back to back intercontinental trips at the drop of a hat. I learned to respectfully but firmly state my point of view when I disagreed, manage the conflict between a sense of loyalty and raise concerns outside the team where it was necessary. I had to feel and manage intense anger and attempt to direct it constructively. I had to understand what part of the relationship was my responsibility and what wasn't about me at all. I learned to manage the intense personal disappointment by reassessing my expectations and understanding the boundaries between line management, mentoring and belonging.

I also had to examine and reset how I led my team.. As the management issues reverberated throughout the whole team, I strained even harder to create a safe space for the more junior staff, to be the reliable, accepting, guiding and mentoring one. Some colleagues enjoyed this cushioning, some actually resisted. I remember discussing my management style with Susie. She said to me, 'I'd hate to be managed that way.' That was a real eye-opener moment for me. It prompted me to examine again how my feelings were blinkering me. I wasn't able to see objectively other people's personal styles and preferences. I wasn't creating a space for others to grow in their own way. My own anxiety was smothering people.

The conclusion is about course correction.

All my work experiences, the good ones and the bad ones, especially the bad ones, contributed to my leadership journey. I found it hard to understand and manage my feelings. I had challenges creating safe relationships at work. But I continued to find 'the people' side the most compelling and interesting part of my career. I still very much enjoyed connecting with colleagues, working with others to problem-solve, rallying diverse individuals around a cause. More than anything, despite everything, I still wanted to be a good leader. Until that point, I had learned leadership by "doing", by observing others' good or bad leadership, by working on myself through coaching or psychotherapy. I remained curious about the mechanics of leadership. I felt I was missing a piece of the leadership puzzle. Going back to university to do an Executive MBA was another step in my transformation. It challenged a lot of the assumptions about what I can do. I have always been good at words, not so good at numbers. Putting myself through acounting and corporate finance classes meant I had a second opportunity to develop a growth mentality. I confronted my fear of not being good at it, managed to enjoy the process rather than stress about the outcomes.

The structured leadership journey, that started with MBTI, really helped me understand myself and grow into the leader I am today. I am still working through challenges and wading through difficult feelings, but I feel I have better tools to make sense of myself, my own biases and triggers. One of the mottos that stuck with me from my secondary school Greek was *gnothi seauton* – know thyself. That's the lesson I treasure most from my leadership journey.

CHAPTER EIGHTEEN

Relationships Are the Source of Results

A RESPONSE TO DIANA FROM SUSIE

> One of the criticisms I've faced over the years is that I'm not aggressive enough or assertive enough or maybe somehow, because I'm empathetic, it means I'm weak. I totally rebel against that. I refuse to believe that you cannot be both compassionate and strong.
>
> Jacinda Ardern

Being able to build meaningful relationships at work and more broadly in our career, helps us to learn and "get things done". It's about being emotionally intelligent and aware of what kind of person we are. It's about seeing what is happening around us and the wider environment and culture in which we are operating. The relationships we build in our current role and in the development of our career are integral to our success. And when it comes to our mental health and wellbeing and being able to thrive, studies have shown that having a good support network with strong relationships you can count on is vital.

Gerard, in chapter five, recognises the importance of relationships in both his finance and his medical career. He tells us: 'You build a relationship with your patient in order to understand their story, support them with their journey and help them heal themselves. Business is similar; it's only via the relationships you build that you succeed, gathering the information, and acquiring the right data for decision making.'

Looking inwards

How do we use our emotional response to a situation to guide us and shape our style but balance this with more rational decision making? Diana examines how her powerful emotions have been the driving force of her career, both for good and less good. She explains how these emotions have impacted her choice of career, her response to a given scenario and the strength of her working relationships. However intense, emotional reactions can colour our response to a situation and make us less able to listen to and respond sensitively to others. We want our thinker to be in charge, to recognise and understand our emotional response as vital information but to use our emotions as only part of the evidence when we make decisions. Diana reflects, 'Coaching prompted me to examine again how my feelings were blinkering me. I wasn't able to see objectively other people's personal styles and preferences.' But this is really complex; recognising, managing and then harnessing our emotions at work is really challenging.

Sarah, in chapter twenty-three, attempts to leave her emotions at the office entrance. She expends energy hiding them. She sees emotions as a 'weakness'. Once she understands how she can harness that sensitivity she tells us that it: 'Brings out empathy, understanding and kindness in my leadership style.' Sarah announces: 'It is high time I recognise the value of this sensitive approach, rather than seeing it – or feeling it – as a flaw.' Ami, in chapter three, recognises her tendency to make immediate judgments of others and how this has limited her interactions. She writes: 'I always struggled with office politics, in particular, forming meaningful relationships with colleagues. With a tendency to take people and situations at face value, I struggled to grasp the subtext of certain decisions made in the workplace.' Sarah, Diana and Ami have learnt how to apply and adjust their style so that they can build on the strengths that make them distinctive whilst managing elements of their personality that might sabotage them. This insight has enabled them to make the most of the relationships that they have at work.

Setting relationship intentions

I recently worked with a team of nine, focusing on how they communicate effectively at work. Here is a summary of what they wanted to do differently after the workshop. It's a great example of some of the elements that inhibit the quality of relationships that we build in the office.

Zareen
Think about my physical state/mindset as I approach the interaction
Practise my warm-up
Be more in control of the meeting

Patrick
Managing my first impression
Being more concise

Alan
Leading and driving more conversations

Grace
Being confident to share more new ideas and connect these to the purpose and strategy

Mohammed
Thinking about my role before I start a meeting/call
Thinking about my input more carefully

Rachel
Connecting with 'why' for the client, why for our company, why for me
Increasing my contributions

Antonia
Feeling more confident that I can have a share of voice
Change my language to be more assertive

Aysia
Leading and being more assertive in meetings

Jamie
Taking a pause/being calmer
Connecting meetings with the overall purpose and outcome that the organisation needs

Which of these elements of relationship building in the boxes above resonate with you?

The social elements of your success are all about how we understand and interact with the world around us. We need to understand when we are at our best, and what might sabotage us, but also the context that we work in. What are others' priorities, interests and concerns? This is more about intellectual empathy, if you like. How will you focus on others' perspectives? Learn about your clients and stakeholders? Know which messages will land?

Creating connections in your organisation

Ask yourself:

→ What interest do others have in the outcome of my work in the organisation?

→ What might be the background issues?

→ What motivates them most of all?

→ What information do they want from me?

→ How do they want to receive information from me?

→ Who influences their opinion of me?

Let's look at somebody who is an expert in creating powerful relationships with her clients. My client, Nisrine, is an expert in brand strategy and she needs to understand who her clients are, why they want to work with her company and how her work can add really value. She develops relationships with clients quickly and provides great clarity in her communication. Her knowledge of the client business is always present and she presents her company capabilities in the right way to influence thinking. Nisrine has an ability to structure thoughts in a way that elevates thinking and gets right into the heart of the discussion to create direction that is actionable. She has a brilliant ability to pose the right questions to frame any challenge. She brings excellent strategic thinking into any conversation and drives the team to broaden their perspectives and understanding of client needs. She shares her knowledge of craft and learning regularly and effectively with the team, subtly bringing learning into every conversation she is in. Nisrine is capable of tailoring her style accordingly in any setting. She inspires the team by balancing her role as an advisor with that of a coach, listening intently and empowering individuals to find their way through to their own solutions.

Impressive? These are all aspects of relationship building that that you might recognise as your own superpowers or areas that you want to work on. Nisrine knows and challenges herself to experiment with her style and can adapt and call on a range of these styles to maximise the impact that she makes. She is attuned to how someone is thinking and feeling in the moment and is able to shift position when something isn't landing with the audience. Of course Nisrine also has saboteurs that she is working on!

What type of impact do you make on others? This can take many forms; for some it's about charisma, for others it's a sense of being authentic or a distinctive style of working/leadership?

My client, Euan, received the following feedback:

'You promote your ideas clearly and convincingly.'

'You are persuasive and able to influence others toward a plan of action.'

'You create a sense of excitement and energy in those around you.'

'Your ability to listen is one of the factors that makes you a stealth negotiator.'

Euan was able to make others care about what he said. He made them feel something and could even change their course of action on an issue.

You and your manager

What does a thriving relationship with your manager look like? Somebody who will have a personality style different to you, a unique set of drivers and will have their own subjective picture of reality. Knowing your manager, how do you get the best out of him or her? If your reflections identify that your working relationship needs improvement, don't be discouraged; your one-on-one meetings provide an opportunity to invest in building trust and demonstrating your commitment to your role. What do you want your manager to walk away knowing about you, your performance, what you are working on, and what you are building in your work? Check your assumptions: what assumptions might you be making about them, their behaviour and their goals and priorities?

Designing your life with others

It's very easy to think of career development as a solo activity; getting a CV together, scrolling through online job opportunities, attending the interview. But it's much more of a collaborative process; you won't have all the answers or resources. All the people that you meet, engage, co-create with will be crucial for your future. Talk to others about your current role, what you care about and what your different scenarios for the future might look like. When I work with clients, I ask them to talk to their "community" about their strengths; it's interesting to see who people go to. Community is hard to find today; you may have to create one or even a few. A challenge for you: can you get together with people for an explicit purpose? For example, 'women in sustainability', 'fathers at work', ' flourishing in your sixties'. It's not purely discussing ideas; it's about people talking about their lives openly and honestly and turning up regularly to do so. You can divide your community into sub-groups:

Family

A great source of feedback for you but a health warning here: you know that they may have their own agenda and life view. They may reinforce some of the identities that you are aiming to shed! Remember Sean in Chapter One who recognised the value that his parents put on financial security. Sean reached the stage where he was able to question this value for himself and embark on a riskier way forward.

Close Friends

People who all know you really well and can often stimulate your thinking through challenge as you have high levels of trust between you.

Supporters

Current or past colleagues who can encourage you and give you great feedback.

Mentors

I really recommend you identify people who will give you wise counsel and advice. Some organisations will have an official mentoring system but if this doesn't happen ask people who you identify as interesting for a meet up; perhaps a coffee now or then?

Rlationship that you must manage. You don't want people who just deliver irrelevant advice to you. How can the mentor understand you and your mindset so that they can access their experience but allow you to see a situation in a new light?

But why don't you also reach out beyond your normal community network? If you are looking to change career or find a new role, try building relationships outside your normal circles. Perhaps ex-employees of the company you work for, people you meet in your voluntary work, as a trustee or at a conference. You might be seen differently by these individuals. They can help you shift how you see yourself and the type of opportunity that you might explore. This is where telling your story becomes really important. Take a look at chapter twenty, which will tell you more.

Relationships really do matter. The quality of our time at work, our sense of fulfilment and wellbeing and our ability to cope when things get tough are related to the degree that we are connected to others. It is easy to underestimate the value of making connections, but these relationships are vital for the span of your working life, whatever path you pursue.

CHAPTER NINETEEN

Coming Home

CASSIE

A year ago I had the sense of new beginnings in my life, of change on the horizon. I didn't know how that change was going to happen, but it was clear that it would come. I knew I'd move out of my home of twelve years, to a new house and a different area. I was in the early months of a big new role, as chief executive of a children's reading charity, and I knew that I was just getting started. We were also in the first months of a global pandemic, and although plenty of predictions were being made, no-one knew what the next months would bring.

A year on, with the morning light just about peering through the heavy March sky and onto the desk, I can look back at the last year with some perspective. With the benefit of spring sunshine, and with some major life and work events in the recent past, it feels good to lift my gaze and think about the bigger picture. I might still be living amongst packing boxes, but this is a moment to breathe, to pause, and to consider where I am; at the start of a new chapter.

The last few months have been overwhelming, muddled, and wonderful too. I moved houses twice. Once from a London suburb to a pit-stop in Cornwall, then to a new house in Birmingham – the home town I left nearly thirty years ago. During the same weeks (from six different desks in temporary not-quite-home working spaces) I delivered World Book Day. It was my first year in the driving seat of the major annual celebration to encourage children and families to read. And, with schools and public spaces closed, it was a World Book Day like no other. All in all, the last few weeks were a disruptive, disorienting time when the ground beneath my feet didn't seem completely stable.

But, through all of that time, work, and the drive to do well at work, is a constant presence. It's sometimes reassuringly familiar, sometimes overly demanding, but I know that for me the need to find some meaning through work is always there. It's sometimes an accelerator and sometimes a brake – but it is there no matter where I am or what else is going on around me. This intense experience – of the personal (the move) and professional (moving two weeks before World Book Day) – has given me a chance to reflect on the role work has played in my life, and in shaping who I am today.

The first job I had was in the children's section of a high street shoe shop. I worked only on Saturdays, and I didn't last all that long (I couldn't care enough about whether customers spent an extra 10% on shoe polish or protector. I was always sure they had some at home somewhere). What I remember most was the feeling of independence. I'd head into town on the bus and bringing myself back after a busy day. I'd take my breaks outside – on the benches by the cathedral, with a book, or watching the shoppers – until it was time to measure small feet for another few hours before going home. It was a first step towards understanding that work could empower, but also feel slow and dull if your heart isn't in it. From that early job onwards, I was looking for work that could be meaningful, and where I could make a difference.

I didn't think I'd find it in my hometown. As a teenager I felt uninspired by Birmingham. It seemed dull and grey. I could see other people's pride in the place, but for me it felt constricting and dreary, and I planned to leave. I knew I wanted to become an adult in a different place, and it was just a matter of time. Moving on from Birmingham always seemed possible. My parents had moved to it for their work and my sister had left it for hers. I grew up in family that valued education, progressive thinking, and social justice. We'd visit London all the time for demos, joining crowds of people to march from Speaker's Corner to Trafalgar Square in pursuit of making a point. Then we'd peel off and spend an hour or so in the National Gallery, or the Tate, and just enjoy what London had to offer, before getting back on the coach home to Brum. So it felt reasonable, even necessary, to think of going to university elsewhere, and to plan for the future to take shape in London.

Since I've chosen to come back home to Birmingham I'm now reflecting on how the 18-year-old me would be furious with my choice. That person had ambitions to leave and be successful somewhere else. Why spend years trying to escape a place, only to return?

Coming back to where I grew up (the bus I took to my sixth-form college passes by the end of my road), has inevitably brought back thoughts of what it was like to be young here. I've wandered through parks that I used to hang out in on sunny days. I've walked through the centre of town and mourned the loss of the massive central library building where I'd borrow music and books and 'revise'. I've retraced my steps to old jobs. But when I drive past my old school, and I remember moving between classrooms and through years in those buildings, I remember how I learnt how to swallow ambition, and to keep my head down.

The school didn't expect a lot of me, and I perhaps I didn't expect a lot of it, either. I might have had some romantic ideas about going through the gates of a listed building, looking a little like the boarding schools described in the many and varied 'Third term at Privilege Towers' paperbacks I was so keen on. If I did, the reality of day-to-day life at school soon knocked it out of me. Some early run-ins with older kids and other kids and long-serving teachers gave me the message; just be normal and, whatever you do, don't show off. Any indication that someone might think too much of themselves drew the wrong kind of attention and not much approval, so I made sure not to stand out.

It was a strategy that kept me, mostly, under the radar of the other kids. But it also meant I pretty much passed through under the radar academically too. I was held in the middle band for GCSEs, meaning I was never expected to achieve anything better than straight Cs. So, for quite a while I didn't expect much of myself either.

It wouldn't be fair to forget a couple of teachers who could see through my defences. I remember when Mr Hawker celebrated my 100% in the quadratic equations test – possibly more than I did. And when Mr Webb gave me the responsibility of running the tuck shop (with the dizzying joy of stacking a cash and carry trolley high with boxes of penny chews and crisps). I know that having this kind of support was great for me. At a time when I didn't feel academically capable, and when I thought I might never escape, the encouragement made me feel capable. It fed my sense that working hard could have a value of its own, and it kept my ambition alive.

I was also, and still am, a voracious reader. It has always made me happy to lose myself in a book. Being a reader gave me an identity, and reading let me explore new identities and worlds. I'm happy in the library. I'm happiest in a corner with a book. I'm pretty sociable too, yes, but there is no question that reading (fiction and more fiction) is and was a refuge, a home, an adventure, a place to learn, a place to be, and what has made me, me. Reading was the doorway to an interest in the world around me, told through the arts. There are great stories everywhere, brilliant narratives brought alive through paintings and photography, film, theatre and any other arts experience. Reading was the opening to a world that has brought me so much insight, joy and ideas.

There are four core elements to good stories; plot, people, place, and purpose. In every paperback consumed on the sofa on a Sunday afternoon, or on a train packed to the brim with commuters, every delicious novel I've read, and every film or play too, has been baked from those ingredients. So it'd hardly be surprising if my own way of approaching the world, and work, has been guided by the same. I've absorbed these things; plot, people, place, and purpose and turned them into my own story.

With the indifferent expectations of school, I might have been left with a sense that my own story would have a straightforward plot. A good white-collar job to last me my life and career. But I always had a sense that there would be more for me to do. Even if I couldn't imagine the details ahead, I knew that life could be an adventure. As with any adventure, there have been a few plot twists and pivotal moments here and there have led to new chapters of my own story. These are the moments that have helped me to understand why I'm still literally surrounded by books – both at work and at home.

To get to the first plot twist we need to race through a montage; from schools to sixth form, where I found more freedom and started to explore what I could do and was interested in (as well as some heavy black eyeliner). Then skipping around to summers working on a sunny island where I learned more about independence and earning for myself. And then the pivotal moment when I got better A level results than anyone (myself included) expected. This was a turning point in the possibilities open to me. The grades were good enough to help me change course, both in terms of what I would study and where I might go. It was a plot shift that gave me the confidence to pitch for what I wanted; the chance to work with books, authors, bookshops, editors ... but mostly books. I fixed on getting to a career in publishing and got there.

I loved working in publishing, and I enjoyed being a publicist. To be in a role where it was essential to be a reader, to read anything and everything that was presented, to walk past shelves and be told 'you should probably take a few of these to understand what we're all about', to be given a manuscript and be asked for an opinion. All I had to do was connect amazing books to interested readers – all day. It was pure bliss. I moved from work experience and through some junior roles swiftly, to become a publicity manager in a large company. I was enjoying finding my feet in a career, of being good at something that was so connected to my sense of self.

So the second twist came with maternity leave, and with it a realisation of what work means to me. After four years of living the life I'd been aiming for, I found I was married and about to become a mum. I was happy; all points in life seemed to be headed in the right direction. But I was worried about leaving work behind. It all felt too new, and too hard-won, to let go of, even for a few months. I was looking forward to being with my baby, and I also micro-managed handover plans and worried about what would happen while I was gone. I expected to feel a pull back to the job – and instead the opposite happened.

Once my daughter arrived, I became fixed on living a life where I could be with her more. Not in an office, not out at work events in the evenings, but able to be a day-to-day presence in her early years. I dreamt up a scheme to run a local café (fondly imagining a peaceful child asleep in sling or bouncy chair somewhere within gazing distance . . .) and I contemplated life with the drop-in salary if I didn't go back to work at all.

Just as the moment to decide – to resign or go back – came along, a letter came through from the Student Loans Company. It reminded me of the massive investment I'd made, with the support of my parents and others, in a future where that education was necessary. With the debt still there, and not likely to be paid back if I wasn't earning, I thought about how important it had been to get to university. Perhaps, with that education behind me, there was more to be achieved?

In coming, reluctantly, back from leave, I found a compelling and clear sense that I wanted more from my working life. At first, and at various times ahead, it felt heavy and heartbreaking not to be around as much as other mums were. I knew that if I was going to be away from my daughter every day, work had to be fulfilling. I had to make more of what I'd reached for in the first place. I refound my drive, and ambition, and a few months after returning was promoted to a new, more interesting and more demanding role. I could be a parent, and I could build my career too. I could love my daughter, and I could learn and grow as an individual. I could dedicate my time and attention to work. I could pull off a good birthday party and would need to miss Sports Day sometimes. These two sides of life aren't incompatible – but it has taken a lot of learning and to get the balance somewhere close to right (and I'm still not sure I get it right, even though now she's 18).

I hope I don't approach every day like I'm at the centre of my own airport paperback thriller, but I do know that absorbing so many tales allowed me to visualise different ways of doing things. My drive to learn more, and to explore every new chapter, comes from knowing that there can be more to a story than first meets the eye. I did, and do, feel the need to explore what could be next, or new, and what I'll learn from the next thrilling instalment of life.

People, characters, are essential to a great story. I know that reading helped me observe other lives and develop an empathy for what someone else might be feeling or thinking. Working well with people is all about seeing others' perspective and motivation. In a team every individual is bringing different elements to make the story live and breathe.

Whenever I come across a sticky moment there is a cast of characters I can refer to for advice. I can think about how one person would have negotiated a complex problem with humour and resilience, or how another's blend of integrity and drive would have motivated a new team. I have had the challenge of leading teams when the snarky influence of one person is souring the efforts of everyone around them. And I've known one person's enthusiasm and expertise to lift a whole team's effort. Either way, it has always helped to get to know people, where they're coming from, and more about their approach to work. When a new personality enters the room, I wonder who they are and where their arrival will take us all. If I understand what lies behind someone's actions perhaps we'll work well together (or perhaps I'll understand why we won't). It's a technique that doesn't stop people being sometimes baffling and sometimes frustrating, but it helps to understand that, just like the best characters, everyone is driven by their own sense of purpose and our collective story is played out together.

Thinking about people, and trying to understand their stories, has allowed me to reflect more on my role as a leader and understand that I prefer to find strengths and the common threads that bring us together. Because I've trusted people more when they've brought more of themselves to work, I feel more comfortable – and like I'm a better leader – when I do the same.

It took a while for me to appreciate what my character can bring to a story. With the secondary school experience ringing too loudly in my ears, I spent years with a reluctance to step forward and with a fear of showing off, or of making any impact as a strong character myself. The process of coaching, and learning from good leaders, helped me see that what I had was worth offering. I feel it less now – but not never. In writing this I keep meeting a very uncomfortable sense that I'm doing something sort of distasteful, a bit embarrassingly self-regarding ... but now I try to understand that fear as a sign of needing to explore the detail of what's making me uncomfortable or clashing with my values. Sometimes I might even enjoy a little showing off, now that I know that I can be good at presenting myself and my ideas, and can do well at bringing people together.

Place, another core element, can mean a few things. When I think about geography, I know the best job I ever had was working in a pub – where I could look out at the sea every time I took out pasty and chips for a table of six, and collected the empty pint glasses later. But place isn't all about the buildings or the spaces. It's more about the work-places, the organisations and cultures, the different characteristics that shape both how we interact, and how at home we feel.

Early in my publishing years I took a short detour to a PR agency. There was something about the culture there that felt all wrong. There was nothing specific about the people, or the building, or the job, but after three months I knew things weren't right. I went back into an in-house publishing job as soon as I could. I was more at home with the books and the editors and designers around me, and I realised how vital it was for me, at the time, to be part of an organisational culture that valued the whole machine of making books.

The challenge I'm enjoying most about my World Book Day role is the arm-band-less weirdness of leading a whole organisation and of bringing together a new team of people. It's a small charity that has, for years, done a massive amount on no staff at all. As the first CEO it's my job to build the organisation around the successful event. At first, I was the only employee, and over the year of lockdown we have grown to a massive four members of staff. It is exhilarating to think that it is up to us to set and shape the culture, and to define and live the values of the organisation.

We are a small enough team to not need an office of our own. Even if we weren't required to work from home, most of us would prefer to. In the short time – less than a year – that we've been together we've navigated the currents of personality and professional expertise. We've decided to be respectful of each other's strengths and vulnerabilities, ambitious in what we want to achieve and mindful of when we need to breathe. We support each other, and it feels like fun. Without a door or desks or a place to make tea we've delivered some impressive work and are creating a culture and a place that we can be proud of.

The World Book Day team's sense of place is created by our shared purpose. So we share the fourth core element of storytelling, and it helps create our place and culture. We share a commitment to the purpose of encouraging children and families to read, because of the impact reading can have on everyone's lives. We are all dedicated to doing a good job – and to improving the outcome every time. As individuals though, we do have different motivations. Ultimately this will take us off in different directions and to do different things. When someone heads off to their new role, they will (hopefully) be replaced on the cast list by someone else who shares our collective purpose.

Most of the time I feel very fortunate to have always had a strong sense of purpose. I know it has driven and guided me, towards and in whatever I've done. From the tuck shop to the shoe shop, from publishing through to World Book Day, it is knowing I could make a difference (or not) that has drawn me in (or left me cold). I am motivated by knowing my efforts will create change and improve things. Now, as a charity CEO, that sense of social justice can come through more clearly too. Reading will improve life chances – and I am committed to that vision. Having a purpose took me from a childhood love of books and reading into sharing that love of books and reading with others. My sense of wanting to explore the world of arts and culture, and give something useful to it, gave me a purpose when it was difficult to find meaning in the organisations I worked for and the culture around me.

This purpose has given me internal expectations that can be a powerful driver, a positive force for learning more and doing things better. A sense of purpose has encouraged me to move on into new roles and organisations. It has been part of why I've been able to develop and grow into my own character and leadership, while I worked out what my own strengths and flaws are, and what my unique contribution can be.

But purpose can also be a hard taskmaster, setting some high expectations of what success, or productive, or good looks like. I know that it can derail me when I feel the goal wasn't quite reached. It can mean that sometimes success at work is too closely linked to how I feel about myself. I've learned that I need to remind myself to stop and celebrate a success – instead of rushing on to the next, to see what can be done better next time.

So, all four elements of a story are part of this present chapter, looking out of the window of this new house, and of why I can come back to Birmingham looking forward to the future.

At this stage in the plot, on this new page, I'm moving out of the confusion and disorientation of moving to a new house and settling into the second year of a role. It's beginning to feel like I belong – in both the house and the job. Setting up shelves and unpacking books was, not surprisingly, a good step to feeling more at home.

Birmingham feels like the right choice. There are new things to explore and benefits to being here. It feels liberating to be away from a daily commute, and to gather some time back for life (and reading). In the last year expectations of how we run our working lives have been turned upside down. I can run an organisation in a city outside London, and with much more of a balance between work and life. Moving out of London house prices means I'm more financially free too. In the future I'll have more autonomy to make choices, and to explore where my professional life might take me. Having this foundation means I can be more authentically me at work and more successfully me outside of work too.

And I know I'm back here in a different version of myself. I'm here on my own terms, and with enough self-knowledge to reassure the younger me – to answer her 'why on earth are you back here?' question with understanding and compassion. It's easy to answer because I see her ambition, that drive to do more and better, in the grown-up person too. There will be even more exciting times around the corner.

Birmingham had seemed like a place to escape from, and now it represents an exciting future. I had been keen to leave behind a city that felt tired and grey. Now it feels dynamic and ready to burst into life. The City of Birmingham crest is on the street name outside the house. It greets me every time I turn towards the front door. There are two figures; a man holding a hammer, symbolising industry, and a woman holding a book and painter's palette, representing art. The motto of this city is 'Forward'. It feels good to be here.

CHAPTER TWENTY

So, Tell me About Yourself? Using Your Life Story to Create Career Change

A RESPONSE TO CASSIE FROM SUSIE

> You're never going to kill storytelling, because it's built in the human plan. We come with it.
>
> Margaret Atwood

M y clients who have written their stories in this book have deeply reflected, debated and then been fantastically brave to document the story of their working lives for you. Has this helped you to reflect on your own career story? What resonates with you? Inspires you? Allows you to understand your own value or your vulnerabilities? How can you use the story to inspire those around you and create the change you want to make happen? We know that when we are undergoing a shift in our work identity we have to try stuff and experiment. We want others to understand who we are and what we have to offer. This is where the story becomes so important. A great recounting of your story needs you to be aware of who you are right now. And Cassie tells us that: 'There are four core elements to good stories: plot, people, place, and purpose.'

Psychologists have shown just how our interpretations of memories can alter our future behaviour. In an experiment published in 2005 (i), researchers had college students who described themselves as socially awkward in high school recall one of their most embarrassing moments. Half of the students reimagined the humiliation in the first person, and the other half pictured it in the third person. Two clear differences emerged. Those who replayed the scene in the third person rated themselves as having changed significantly since high school – much more so than the first-person group did. The third-person perspective allowed people to reflect on the meaning of their social miscues, the authors suggest, and thus to perceive more psychological growth.

A client I was working with this week had a bit of an "aha" moment. Garvesh was brought up in Nepal by two teachers and now works in risk management in a bank. How could these careers be connected? But he is at his happiest when facilitating workshops, sharing his expertise with those less experienced and coaching others to develop. The feedback he receives is all about the impact that he makes with these initiatives, and this is what really differentiates him in his role. It's the reason he will get promoted. More importantly, it's the reason why his job feels meaningful. How can he build on these strengths in the future? Does it matter that he identified that these were the strengths that his parents have? He told me that he loves the idea of their legacy or gift to him and this understanding has now opened him up to new work possibilities.

It's the story we tell

How well can you talk about your working life? Can you explain to others why you made the decisions that you did? How has your childhood and education impacted the person who now shows up at the office? What have you learnt about what motivates you? When are you at your best?

If you haven't already done this exercise, have a go at the lifeline exercise in Appendix B. When you have drawn your timeline, have a go at telling this story to others; explore what is emerging as key themes of your working life. Caveat here, this is difficult! It's difficult because it's hard to disentangle what's really important for your audience. It's very tempting to give a chronological account of your life which will actually just end up being exactly what you would write on a CV. Step away and imagine your life as a series of newspaper headlines. What are the big themes that connect you to your audience? Where will you start? What might your audience be looking for? How might your experience match this?

Garvesh could begin his story by explaining that there is a central theme that connects all his work. This is the theme of knowledge sharing, developing expertise in others and facilitating learning. He could then explain how he does this in his present role but also how his experience, education and cultural background all contribute to these strengths. He would weave in how he builds relationships, what values drive his behaviour and how he uses his type of intellect to solve problems. His audience will want to understand what is the most meaningful way he can contribute to the organisation.

To support the timeline exercise, take a big piece of paper and create some 'theme' bubbles of your own. The story can be used in many ways. Try to distill it into a maximum three-minute account. This can then be used for interview questions such as: 'Tell me more about yourself? Tell me why you applied for this role?' Or it can be used when you are meeting somebody new in your organisation, having a session with a new mentor, meeting a new team member or a manager. You will obviously have to edit and shift pieces according to your audience. People might want to know about a specific piece of expertise but they also may want to understand what are your more generic strengths.

Developing helpful tools

Many of my clients create an online presentation which allows them to expand on their CV and is more like a story. It will contain pages such as: what were my early influences? What is my career timeline? What are the three top ways that I add value at work? Perhaps there is a case study to illustrate this and a page detailing feedback from others on the client's strengths. This is a clever way to understand your reputation, how others see you. It may better help you to understand your value. Below is an example; these words helped the client find the right language to talk about himself and what he did really well.

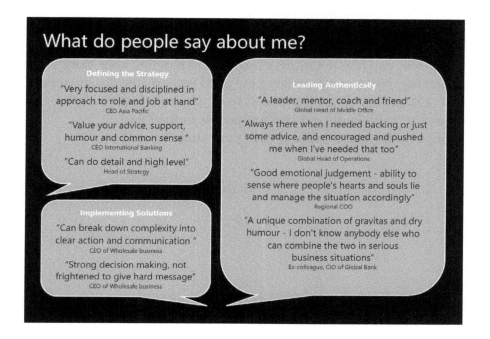

This is especially relevant when you are moving into a new area of the organisation or changing career. I supported a lawyer, Julie, who wanted to move into brand strategy. It was a challenge to extract commonalities between the strengths both required. Julie identified that analytical thinking and research, business development, building client relationships and project management were needed in both roles. She then crafted a story using these themes and pulling out her other recognised strengths of strategic thinking and creativity that she wanted to bring to brand strategy.

Back to Garvesh from Nepal. A warm and talented man who found it uncomfortable to tell others how good he was. Is this something you find challenging? This is very common and may have roots in our culture, gender, "showing off" norms or even our own inner self critic. After all humility is one of the cornerstones of great leadership.I have seen real differences in cultural norms around assertiveness and this holds back talented people from getting promoted. Crafting your story carefully will give you more confidence to detail the nuances of your experience and explain how your work makes an impact. This is the key part; your audience wants to hear what difference you make, not necessarily how wonderful you are, so this may help you to redefine your story. And remember: if you don't explain how good you are, the wrong person will get that job, or that new role. Gutting for you and the organisation will not have the best people in the role.

So, over to you; good luck with your story telling!

CHAPTER TWENTY-ONE

My Inner Saboteur and Me

CATHAL

When I was fifteen I told a friend of mine, 'I'm going to be a director when I get older.' With one cynical eyebrow raised he replied, 'What are you gonna direct? Traffic?' Being a sensitive adolescent I greeted this with an expletive followed by 'off' and explained to my witty mate that, no, I'm not planning to direct traffic; I'm planning to direct films. He seemed momentarily and moderately intrigued, maybe even impressed, and he gave me as much encouragement as he could muster: 'You're an awful eejit sometimes, d'ya know that? Do you have any cigarettes on ya?' I may have been mistaken about how impressed he was.

Nearly twenty-five years on as my dreaded 40th birthday approaches, I have yet to direct one single film; not a short, not a feature, not a documentary, not a mockumentary – nothing. As I got older my youthful film-making fantasy was overwhelmed with adult reality. *How do you even begin to make a film?* I'd ask myself as I studied English and Psychology in university, a degree I chose because it seemed to be the sensible option at the time (plus my exam results in school weren't good enough to get into the one film school that existed in Ireland in the early 2000s). My confidence gave way to doubt in pursuit of my dream and my excuses came thick and fast.

'I can't afford to rent film equipment, never mind buy any.'

'Write a screenplay? Are you joking? Do you know how long those things are?'

'Even if I did write something, and even if I did manage to shoot something, how the hell could I edit it?

'Even if I did figure out how to edit it, then what? Who'd want to look at it?'

As legendary drag queen Ru Paul would have observed, 'Your inner saboteur is in full control'; and my outer-self was putting up little resistance. I'm not sure exactly where my inner saboteur gets its power, but incredible power is what it has and it knows exactly how to wield it. And as long as I can remember it's always been there.

For example, when I was eight years old all I really wanted was to be like my older brother. He played basketball, so I played basketball. He collected Lego, so I collected Lego. And he, like nearly every other boy over the age of ten in our primary school in late '80s small-town Ireland, was an altar boy. So, you guessed it, I wanted to be an altar boy (or a "server" as we were called in our parish). After quite a lot of nagging on my part, my brother asked his best friend – who was a server team captain in need of an extra team member – to train me up despite my young age (yes there were teams of altar boys and yes, those teams had captains). Notwithstanding this low-level form of nepotism, I was thrilled. All I could think was, *I'm going to be on the actual altar during actual Mass. I'm going to wear special server's garments* (awful black & white, scratchy polyester robes). *I'm going to hold the burning incense contraption before the priest would shake it at a coffin.* And most importantly, *I'm gonna be like my big brother.*

The next day my brother's friend, who was all of eleven years old, came up to me in the school playground during break and said he'd meet me at the church this Saturday at 10am to give me my first training session as a Mass server. Slightly intimidated but full of beans, I told him I'd be there.

When Saturday morning arrived a certain unease began to rise in me. I was suddenly incredibly apprehensive about going to the church to begin training. At that point the prospect of smelling the incense made me feel ill. As the clock ticked closer to ten the more apprehensive I became. I hadn't told my brother or my parents exactly when I was to meet the team captain. The feeling that was rising inside me seemed to be telling me, *Don't go.* It whispered, *Just keep quiet and no one will know.* My inner saboteur had taken hold of the controls. *Just keep watching cartoons.* 10am came and went and I still sat in front of the TV. My apprehension gave way to relief. It then rapidly gave way to intense guilt. I was thinking about my brother's friend (who was a genuinely nice person, not intimidating at all) waiting for me in the cold rain outside the church oblivious to the fact that my inner saboteur didn't give a shit if he got cold *or* wet.

But what did my inner saboteur want from eight-year-old me? And what do they want from nearly-forty-year-old-me? And why do I give in to it so often?

As my three-year BA was coming to an end the realisation that it was not going to lead me to an obvious career path was seeping in. I was facing the first September of my life with zero plans. Septembers had been curated for me for twenty-one years. Was I now all of a sudden supposed to decide by myself what to do for this particular September? Apparently so. I decided that after spending three years of phoning in a mediocre degree the best thing to do now was … another degree; a Master's degree to be precise.

The only Master's that I was tempted by was the one in screenwriting. It was a brand new course at my university and I was genuinely giddy about the prospect of being one of its first students. This would finally be the moment where I grabbed the nettle of my film-making ambition. I would learn what it takes to create the perfect screenplay. I would be amongst my Robert Altman-loving peers. I would break all the rules of the traditional three-act structure to create my own, new, revolutionary way of writing films. I would show my cynical, doubting, fifteen-year-old school 'friend' that I would indeed work in film. The movie industry would not know what hit it.

Of course, that would have all quickly materialised if I had actually been accepted for the screenwriting MA. It turned out I was not. I was gutted. I wanted to give up after falling at the first hurdle. I'd been chewed up and spat out. Actually, I hadn't even been chewed up. I hadn't even made it to the mouth of the film industry. I barely registered as a tempting, smelling morsel to be nibbled on. I was an unappetising and inedible amuse-bouche.

But wait, what's this? I had a second-choice MA application registered. I had been so drunk on the self-entitled delusion of getting into the screenwriting course that I had totally forgotten that I had submitted an application for a back-up course. But what the hell was this course? What other subject would I have dared apply for? More to the point, what other department was willing to accept me? This back-up course was for a Master's degree in ... Drama and Theatre Studies.

OK. Interesting. Theatre? It wasn't my first love, I have to admit; maybe not even my second, or third, or fourth for that matter. I'd probably seen about six plays in my life up to that stage and I'd definitely fallen asleep during at least two of them. But I thought ...

I guess it's kind of similar to film, but with less attractive actors.

And there is a writing module that maybe I could learn something from.

This will just be a detour. I'm taking the scenic route to movie success.

And, well, what other option do I have?

I arrived back at university for day one of my theatre MA in September 2004 with that twisted combination of cynicism and optimism.

Over the following year I saw about thirty theatre shows (I stayed awake for all of them), read dozens of plays and learned a huge amount about the history of Irish theatre and beyond. Crucially, I also wrote and directed a short play as part of a public showcase of new work from students. For some reason creating this play seemed significantly less daunting than the idea of creating a short film. My excuses did not come thick and fast. I think this was partly due to the fact that I was less precious about it. I had watched so many great films through my teens that I had set the bar way too high by comparing myself to expert filmmakers who had been doing it for years. With theatre I kind of didn't know any better. My naivety was liberating. I felt unencumbered by the burden of expectation or comparison.

Perhaps this heavy feeling of expectation and comparison was what kept me watching cartoons that Saturday morning when I was eight instead of turning up at the church. I was scared about not living up to the standards of my brother. If I didn't turn up then the comparison couldn't be made. It wasn't exactly a well-thought out plan but it's something you could forgive a young boy for (as my parents and my brother and my brother's friend did at the time when they found out what I'd done). But as an adult that thinking is not as easy for others to accept. It's not easy for *me to* accept either. I still find myself in a similarly emotionally paralysed place, especially when it comes to work, time and time again. But, when it came to making this short play in university, thankfully, I was, for the most part, free of that.

Also, practically speaking, making a play just felt much clearer than making a film. Everything one needed was pretty much already in place at the university.

A small performance space: Check.
A lighting rig: Check.
A sound desk: Check.
Seats for the audience to sit on: Check.
An endless supply of very eager student actors who were willing to perform the pretentious drivel that I had written: Check.

It was all quite basic but it was there, so therefore it felt clear. It felt achievable.

And people turned up to watch it. Granted, the forty or so audience members who attended were mainly friends, family and the other students. But they had turned up to see what I (and others) had created. That felt good.

Theatre felt clear. Film felt out of focus.

That short play came and went. It was difficult to make and it wasn't particularly good but I didn't burn the theatre down in the process of making it. I felt, in a very small way, vindicated for telling my school friend that I was going to be a director, no matter what happened after that. I felt that, at least for now, my inner saboteur had been pacified.

When September 2005 rolled around and my MA was coming to an end I had the same sinking feeling as I had had twelve months previously. With no obvious career path showing itself I was staring into that familiar abyss of post-university life. There were no more degrees to apply for. I was working at a computer game shop to pay my way and if I wasn't careful I could have remained there for years. I needed to get proactive if being a director was going to become a reality. The title of the job that I was pursuing hadn't changed since I was fifteen. I still wanted to be a director. But one thing *had* changed; I knew it wasn't going to be in film. That one year doing a Master's that I had forgotten I had applied for shifted the entire focus of my working life (well, at least shifted the focus from film to theatre). Theatre had accidentally revealed itself to be the medium that I was compelled to work in, the medium I was best suited to and the medium that had now become my first love.

So, I was clear on the "what". Now I just had to figure out the "how".

One slow day in the computer game shop, I made a list of every theatre company in the country (it didn't take long as there were about six fully funded companies in Ireland). I rang each of them asking if they could offer me any work experience. This proved fruitless. It turns out that an inexperienced, young director with two degrees who's made one ropey short play isn't massively in demand in a tiny theatre market that's already over-saturated. This was another hurdle I tripped on and I had that sinking feeling again. I didn't want to drag myself up, dust myself off and try again. I wanted to just sit and watch cartoons.

About eight months later I was in the back garden of my parents' house in rural Ireland playing basketball by myself when my Nokia 1325 rang. I didn't recognise the number but I answered none the less. The deep voice on the other end said, 'Hi, it's Mike Diskin.' Mike was a notoriously brusque yet charismatic man who ran the Town Hall Theatre in Galway City at that time. He was influential and, despite his no-bullshit demeanour, generous to younger theatre makers. He was in the process of organising an arts festival called Project '06. Its remit was to programme

Galway-based artists in pop-up venues across the city as a direct response to the fact that the city's international festival was ignoring these local creatives.

So, why was he calling me?

Well, Mike was in a bit of a pickle. One of the plays he had programmed for Project '06 was due to open in twenty days' time but the director had just bailed. Mike didn't want to cancel the production because tickets were already selling. At this stage I had directed my one-act play in university and a pretty disastrous, zero-budget, amateur production of David Mamet's Glengarry Glen Ross (with Irish accents!). Also, out of all the people in Galway who called themselves a theatre director, I was about the only one who didn't have a show on in this festival. A friend of mine who was doing admin work for Mike had seen my university short play and recommended me to fill this directorial breach. She also knew I would definitely be available.

So, that's why Mike was calling me.

'Will you do it?' he asked with a tinge of insistence. Despite the fact that that familiar fear was rising inside of me at the prospect of saying yes, I was also quite fearful of Mike. When he could sense me wavering he said, 'I'll owe you.' Just to be clear, this "job" he was offering me was totally unpaid. A recurring theme of working in the theatre industry is offers of unpaid or very badly paid gigs. So, what exactly he was going to owe me was decidedly unclear. But at that stage of my life I was pretty directionless (and for someone who called themselves a director, that was a particularly damning flaw). I hadn't yet paid my dues. I needed the experience. I needed to test myself. I needed to prove myself. I needed to show up, not just for Mike or for my brother's friend or my parents but I needed to show up for myself.

'I'll do it.'

Thankfully, I had just enough clarity of thought that this was a win-win scenario for me. If I pulled this off by getting the play on in twenty days then I'd have even more leverage with Mike for future projects. But if the show turned out to be a disaster, well, I could always say, 'It wasn't my fault. I was brought in at the last minute.

That other director abandoned the production.' Plus, Mike would – in his words – owe me. So, win-win! I was on my way to Galway the next day to meet the young cast.

Despite the serious reservations I had about agreeing to the project, despite the fact that I didn't know any of the actors, despite the fact that I still had no real clue what a "real" director actually does, this production went well. Over the next two years I and three of the actors who I met on that show started and ran a small theatre company. Mike was true to his word. He gave us generous deals to use his theatre. We staged five productions with each one enhancing the reputation of the company and my experience and skills as a director.

This level of productivity felt rare to me. This unquestionable commitment to getting the work done felt very rare to me. My relationship with consistent hard work has always been a fraught one. Looking back, I spent my primary school years being a relatively smart, reliable and well-behaved pupil without ever needing to put too much effort in. I was always in the top ten percentile in all subjects and I felt comfortable there. My comfort and confidence began to be chipped away, however, as I began to be bullied by some of the "alpha" kids in my class. This continued for about two years and it left its mark. My reaction to this was to hide, sometimes literally. But also I hid away my self-belief and my sense of purpose. My goal, even after the bullies stopped paying me any attention, was to get through the day without drawing too much attention to myself and hopefully I wouldn't feel worthless by the time I went to bed.

As I entered secondary school I noticed that I was slipping down the academic pecking order. More effort was needed to remain in that upper echelon and I was struggling massively to apply that effort. I was more interested in trying to feel safe than striving for the best. My work ethic was questionable at best and my productivity came in fits and starts. There was, however, one glaring exception to this.

In Ireland everyone sits state exams, at around fifteen, called the Junior Cert. It has no bearing whatsoever on future university places or any third-level pursuits. The Junior Cert is strange, stressful and, academically speaking, an inconsequential experience. This was all true for me as much as anyone except when it came to the art exam. The way art was evaluated for the Junior Cert in the 90s was through the creation of a portfolio across the school year. The brief was to create a series of completed pieces in paint, ceramics, print, etc. and display all preparatory and development work. I began this project without a second's thought. I did the bare minimum for other subjects in order to concentrate on my portfolio. Hours were spent in my bedroom immersed in the work. Some time in November of that year, months before anything was due, my art teacher noticed the growing stack of finished pieces that I had. She asked if she could look through them. She then told the rest of the class to gather round. She laid out of each of my completed pieces, one by one, for everyone else to see without saying much. Everyone else in the class had very little done and I think she wanted to scare them into action. She said to me, 'Well done. Keep going,' and she moved on.

I was proud of myself in that moment. I also realised I had done the work because I wanted to, not because I was being forced to. My teacher didn't need to be my taskmaster. I had achieved "flow" while creating that art at fifteen. And I achieved "flow" by directing five plays in two years for my little theatre company in Galway when I was 25. These states of flow are rare. It's not to say I didn't have numerous moments of overwhelming doubt, bad choices and self-flagellation through both experiences. But both were achieved through an early compulsion to lean in to the challenge and I reaped the rewards.

By the end of 2008 I had begun to feel a certain amount of frustration and burnout from running the theatre company. Frustration because the big industry gatekeepers and decision-makers weren't paying us much attention, and burnout because there's only so much theatre one can create on the back of bare minimum funding and endless favours. I also still had a huge amount to learn about directing that just wasn't going to happen in isolation. I made the difficult yet obvious decision to make the move to London. It was the biggest theatre town in the world and it was on my doorstep. I was terrified, but I had hit a glass ceiling in Galway and if I was going to progress as an artist and attempt to turn directing into a functioning career I needed to learn from the best. I moved and gave myself a goal; get on the theatre industry ladder within two years, and if I didn't achieve this, then I'd reassess. I had absolutely no contacts in the London theatre industry when I arrived. I didn't know the names of most of theatres, never mind the people who ran them. But I had a certain sense of arrogant expectation. I thought, *once they realise how much directing I've done they'll throw the doors open and usher me into steady theatrical employment*. This was not the case. Once again, my rather delusional expectations were mismatched by reality. The London theatre industry was awash with people like me, elbowing each other out of the way, desperate to get to the front of the queue for any opportunity.

I spent the first year working in a call centre and volunteering to direct for every one-act festival, pub theatre showcase and rehearsed reading that I could find. Despite building up a small list of unpaid London credits, the feeling of futility was beginning to permeate through me. Once again I was knocking on the door of the big theatres and no one was answering. My inner saboteur was reawakening, I was a long way from having "flow" and the thought of another shift in the call centre was not exactly helping. I was ready to return to Galway. I was ready to return to a familiar, safe place where I didn't have to try very hard. I was ready to give up.

Like many things in my life I procrastinated on my giving-up on London, and lucky for me that I did. During the time that I should have been booking my flight home and giving my notice to my landlord I received an email from the Young Vic theatre, THE directors' theatre in London. I had applied to join their online network of young directors where they exclusively advertise in-house jobs and opportunities that otherwise I would be oblivious to. It had been a couple of months since I submitted my application to be part of this network, and a few weeks since I unsuccessfully chased them for an answer. I had presumed I had failed to be accepted. But better late than never; they said because of my impressive directorial experience I was an ideal person to join the network. THIS. CHANGED. EVERYTHING.

Within three months of receiving that email I applied for an assistant director job at the Young Vic, advertised to just those on their network. There was a week-long interview/workshop process where ten young directors including myself worked with the director and designer testing some ideas for the show. On the back of this I was offered the job. I think what helped set me apart from the other directors was my age and experience. Most of the people I was up against were precocious and very knowledgeable about the industry, as most of them grew up in London and immersed in theatre, but they were a couple of years younger than me and they had directed very little. I've a feeling I was just a little more comfortable in my own skin and the director of the show recognised that. Once I had the job I asked him why he had selected me. He said, 'You knew when to speak up. And you knew when to shut up.' This is something I've been attempting to do in every aspect of my life ever since.

The vast majority of what I apply today in my work, and have applied for the last ten years, I learned on that job. The director included me at every stage of the process and I felt integral throughout. My self-esteem was on the rise and I could feel my foot on that industry ladder's first rung. But I needed to actually direct a London production myself to that ensure my artistic progression, as well as my career progression, moved to the next level too.

I applied for a highly sought-after director's award for under-thirties which granted the winning applicant the funds to direct a studio production at one of London's most prestigious theatres. After three intense rounds of presentations, interviews and workshops I went away feeling like I had represented myself well. I supported and reassured myself through heavy moments of doubt and panic. One week later I was in Tooting Broadway Wetherspoons when I received a call from one of the judges. Miraculously, they told me I'd won. That call came two and a half years after I'd left Galway. It felt more than enough vindication for making the move to London. The third time in my life that I have a distinct memory of achieving "flow" was directing my chosen play, *Disco Pigs* by Enda Walsh, for this award. I worked with brilliant designers, I found the perfect actors, my producer was a close friend who cared for the project as much as I did, I worked hard and I trusted my instincts. It all paid off. The project was a creative and critical success. The original cast, Cillian Murphy and Eileen Walsh, came to see it with the writer and they approved.

Looking back at these achievements – the art project in school, running my theatre company in Galway, directing my first professional production in London – I can reassure myself that I have the capacity to succeed in what I set out to do; that I can achieve flow. However, despite these and other achievements throughout my career I have also displayed a potent and consistent ability to undermine my progress with self-sabotaging behaviour. On more than one occasion I've allowed complacency, insecurity and fear to control my decision-making and cloud my judgement. I've seen golden opportunities slip through my fingers because of immature behaviour and a lack of self-belief. My ambition can propel me to a place of opportunity but my lack of confidence can scupper the potential of that opportunity. Ultimately all this behaviour *is* my inner saboteur. It's the emotional behaviour I displayed as an aspiring eight-year-old altar boy and it's the emotional behaviour I can and have displayed as a thirty-something theatre director. The question is, can I change this behaviour?

This week I visited my recently vaccinated parents for the first time in eighteen months. It was wonderful to be in their company again and a relief to know they're healthy and protected. My mother, through boredom at some stage during lockdown, found the school end-of-year report cards belonging to me and my siblings. Cringing but fascinated I read mine. The consistent observations from each teacher were that I was 'mannerly', 'intelligent', 'sensitive' and 'he needs to work harder to fulfil his potential.' As I approach my 40th birthday I think I'm finally in a place where I can read those words and let them motivate me to improve rather than condemn me to fail. Before, I took them as reflections of the make up of my character that could not change. Deep inside me, I had decided that *is* who I was and that I would never fulfil my potential. Now, I'm ready to soothe my inner saboteur, I'm ready to befriend and understand my inner saboteur. I'm ready to take care of the eight-year-old me and the fifteen-year-old me. I'm ready take responsibility for their ambitions and dreams and do everything I can do make them become a reality. I won't fail them. I won't fail myself.

CHAPTER TWENTY-TWO

Procrastination or Perfectionism?

A RESPONSE TO CATHAL FROM SUSIE

> Perfectionism and procrastination have such a fine line. You say, 'Well, I want it to be good. I want it to be perfect.' But what you're really doing is not doing your work. You're putting off showing up and being visible because then you're going to be judged, and it might suck.
>
> Jen Sincero

How impressed we are by our friends and colleagues who manage to get everything done. Those people who move seamlessly between training for a triathlon, completing that part-time Master's, frequent promotions and finishing a prodigious amount of work. We are in awe; in fact, are you one of them? I know I dream of driving myself towards a future "perfect" state when I will have achieved everything that I set myself to do. I am sincere in applying myself to those things that I value but then get swallowed up by an ever lengthening 'to do' or wish list. There is something tough to get your head round here, because we sense that perfecting your 'craft' demands real focus and a degree of blood, sweat and tears. But perfectionism (and the procrastination that results from it), can be the enemy of creativity and productivity. Because perfectionists are so concerned with the outcome being just right, they can become really risk averse which actually inhibits the innovation and creativity. Ironically, successful perfectionist-procrastinators actually succeed in spite of their behaviour not because of it. But working on this perfectionism is more about redefining or rechannelling a strength of ours rather than having to aim for a lesser goal.

I meet many clients who are on the edge of burnout; often because they have set the bar high in terms of the breadth and volume of work they want to get done. The reasons for this are often complex and can be unique to individual circumstance. It's not necessarily about this perfection of the 'craft'. Procrastination might seem the antithesis of perfectionism and indeed a good ponder and reflection period can be revelatory. How many times have you gone for a walk, switching your brain into 'discovery' mode', creating clarity and perspective on that knotty issue? Anne Lamott (i): 'Perfectionism is a mean, frozen form of idealism, while messes are the artist's true friend. What people somehow (inadvertently, I'm sure) forgot to mention when we were children was that we need to make messes in order to find out who we are and why we are here.'

Progress not perfection

When you have bitten off more than you can chew and your diary becomes too overloaded to manage, you can then avoid starting any habit unless we are really sure we can hit the goal everyday. This can lead to procrastination; or you take on only those habits that you can stick to no matter what. Cathal, in the last chapter, explains to us what it feels like to have the desire to be a theatre director and we read how others recognise this creative talent. When he is 'in the zone' he can be highly productive, but recognises that 'an unquestionable commitment to getting the work done felt very rare to me.' What's going on? For Cathal, it started at school. He explains: 'My comfort and confidence began to be chipped away as I began to be bullied by some of the "alpha" kids in my class. This continued for about two years and it left its mark. My reaction to this was to hide, sometimes literally. But also I hid away my self-belief and my sense of purpose.' Cathal then began to withdraw: 'My goal, even after the bullies stopped paying me any attention, was to get through the day without drawing too much attention to myself and hopefully I wouldn't feel worthless by the time I went to bed.' At work, these feelings became louder and he tells us: 'I've allowed complacency, insecurity and fear to control my decision-making and cloud my judgement.' His harsh self-critic writes: 'I've seen golden opportunities slip through my fingers because of immature behaviour and a lack of self-belief. My ambition can propel me to a place of opportunity, but my lack of confidence can scupper the potential of that opportunity.' A nuanced description of how early life experiences can have profound implications into adulthood. Cathal's procrastination and ability to operate at work can be stymied by a lack of self-belief and fear.

So how might we describe perfectionism? Clinical perfectionists set themselves high, unrelenting, and often unachievable standards in their work or business, and they must reach these goals so that they can maintain a sense of self-worth. According to psychologists Paul Hewitt and Gordon Flett (ii), there are three types of perfectionist: the "self-oriented" type who have strict standards for themselves and are motivated by avoiding failure at all costs; the "other-oriented" type who set perfectionist expectations for others; and the "socially prescribed" form who believe that others expect them to be perfect.

My client, Mina, was described as 'a perfectionist who finds it hard to do something unless it is up to the level she expects. Sometimes this means certain tasks may take her a long time or that she'll be late to a party, but when she gets there, she'll have the perfectly wrapped present.' When Mina was pregnant, she read every possible book on childcare and came up with a piece of work bringing together the best advice from all of the experts. But Mina's perfectionism can be double-edged. It motivates her to do things really well and to do wonderful work. On the other hand, it can cause her anxiety and slow her down. For Mina, although her talents are numerous, she sometimes lacks the confidence to demonstrate them and overthinks, and perfectionism turns into procrastination.

Procrastination or Perfectionism?

> ## REFLECT: Do I have perfectionist tendencies?
>
> Do I tend to focus on the outcome to the exclusion of the process?
>
> Is my satisfaction about the achievement temporary because I sense there is always more to do, be and accomplish?
>
> Do I often beat myself up over any small things that went wrong?
>
> Do I frequently go for a goal and then collapse in exhaustion?

Imperfection is beautiful

When you take an exam, you can achieve that "perfect" score but for most of what you do at work, a perfect outcome was impossible from the outset, there are too many conflicting variables for you to be able to maximise them all. Of course, the fact that life is therefore inevitably a sort of failure applies to absolutely everyone, so in fact should you call it a failure at all? If everyone's guaranteed to miss the target, clearly the issue is with the target. Elizabeth Gilbert (ii) articulates this beautifully: 'We must understand the need for perfectionism is a corrosive waste of time, because nothing is ever beyond criticism. No matter how many hours you spend to render something flawless, somebody will always be able to find fault with it.'

When exploring your next career move, you chat through your ideas with a colleague, friend or coach. You are full of ideas and energy about what you're going to do next. You commit to a deadline for completing your reflections, designing a CV, meeting relevant contacts. Lots of deliverables to move your thinking and actions forward. In your mind, you have great clarity and you can't wait to get started. But as life intrudes, something changes. You want everything to be flawless. Even though you have a vision and great ideas, you keep delaying the start of the process. The excitement that you initially felt begins to feel like dread. *I have to do more research,*

195

gather more information, find more sources of inspiration before I start so it can be really good. I'll get started tomorrow — I've got time, you tell yourself.

Finally, it's the day before you meet your career coach, perhaps that's me! You're now berating yourself for your delay and your sense of self dips along with your drive to act. You're now not only beating yourself up for potentially messing up, but also panicking and stressing to pull it together by the end of the day. The higher your fear of failure, the more you will procrastinate. Again those sabotaging twins appear; perfectionism and procrastination.

Progress not perfection

Procrastination is not about being lazy; it's more often based on a low tolerance for frustration and failure. When people perceive a higher challenge than they feel capable of, they bury this discomfort through a diversionary activity. Researchers led by Sean McCrea of the University of Konstanz in Germany (iv), revealed a cognitive aspect to procrastination; people act promptly when given a concrete task but begin to procrastinate when they view the task in abstract terms. You probably have have times that you decide the kitchen needs cleaning, you begin to scroll randomly through social media or tidy your desk. You delay completing a task that seems like it will take ages, only to realize that it took less time to do it than to repeatedly think about it. Cathal can be held back by his lack of confidence and fear of imperfection; which then makes him less focused. But procrastination could also be about a confusion around what's important or a more complicated anxiousness around the task.

REFLECT

So, what can you do about lack of focus? Here are some hacks:

- Take the task and break it into smaller pieces or steps.
- Give yourself five or ten minutes of focused time.
- Employ the pomodoro technique. This is about having a set amount of time with one segment being a "sprint" and the other a rest. Pomodoro uses 30 minutes with 25 minutes for the sprint, and 5 minutes for the break.
- Build in your own breaks but chunk up your tasks. For example, responding to 10 emails, or doing a 15 minute sprint, or working until a certain time. Stick with it, and reward yourself at the end.
- A single day for a single task: try doing one task, for a certain day. Make sure it's in your calendar and stick to it.

Many perfectionistic tendencies are rooted in fear and insecurity. My client, Ade, works in a prestigious global consultancy. He has worked ferociously and his effort and talents have allowed him to be promoted to a senior role. His colleagues are predominantly from an Oxbridge or Ivy League background (unlike him); he worries if he lets go of his meticulousness and conscientiousness, it will damage his performance and standing. He clings to this perfectionism even when it's counterproductive. When conventional self-discipline turns into compulsion, perfectionists may actually be held back by it. Ade fears that not meeting the goals that he has set himself might mean that there is something unworthy inside of him.

Beginning takes courage

Can you shift to becoming a diligent worker by creating a list of all the things that make your life worthwhile, at home and in work? Ask a close friend or partner to do the same and take a look to see if there are any differences in how you see things. Maybe a pie chart?

Next, think through how you spend your time at work. Is there

197

one area that you spend significantly more time on than others? Where can you put "stop signals" – such as a three-hour time limit – in place to reduce the time spent on that activity? Stop signals are warning signs that you have done enough. They are based on what is reasonable for the job, rather than what will make you feel differently about your ability and they can really help train your mind to move away from perfectionism towards becoming a diligent worker. Also, consider how to praise yourself for tasks that have been achieved well and with energy to spare, rather than those that have taken more resources to achieve.

REFLECT: Working on your procrastination/perfectionism

Explore the following questions:

- Why do I value what I am doing? Think about what is motivating me towards a goal. Have a read of Chapter … on meaning and purpose.
- Have a go at the best/worst/real exercise: what tasks do I feel compelled to do perfectly that I might be procrastinating on? Write down what could be the Best Case Scenario, the Worst Case Scenario, and what is most likely the Realistic Scenario, which will be neutral.
- Think about the difference between excellence and perfection. Excellence stems from enjoying and learning from an experience and developing confidence from it. In contrast, perfection provokes negative feelings from any perceived 'mistakes' made.

Much of the purpose of the coaching work that I do with my clients is to enable them to develop their conscious self-awareness. To assess their strengths and see how these can be employed to build success and fulfilment, but also to bring their shadows into the foreground. Both procrastination and perfectionism are useful examples of how, when better understood, these saboteurs can be addressed.

CHAPTER TWENTY-THREE

You'll Just Have To Try Harder Next Time

POLLY

I was sitting in my aunt's manicured garden, with the sun beaming down, feeling absolutely great. To my parents' delight, my sister and I had just pulled off their surprise 50th wedding anniversary. I was elated, still reeling with a sense of accomplishment, having completed the London Marathon the weekend before.

It was not long, however, before one of my parents' friends decided to bring me back down to earth: 'We always joked you'd be the one to be pregnant first and we definitely wouldn't have put bets on you having a career!'

This was the moment I should have been beaming with pride. I was 36 and co-owned a successful London marketing agency, but it still did not feel enough. Perhaps it was the lack of a significant other, or children, that always threw a shadow over situations like that. Or maybe it was just because, for some reason, I couldn't ever let myself feel proud and celebrate my career success.

That flippant comment stayed in my head. Was it born from my school years, when my grades didn't match their children's? It brought back the familiar feeling that however much I tried, I would never be quite good enough.

Thinking back on my childhood there is one school day that stands out. The day was dragging like no other and the bell could not ring soon enough. With winter nights drawing in, I was wrapped up warm ready to spend the evening in the local pub. From the age of six I had spent numerous glorious weekends at the local amateur dramatics group, and on this particular night in the pub, the am-dram group was holding the auditions for the Christmas panto which, for me, was the absolute highlight of the season.

Dorothea, the chain-smoking director who had worked in the West End, commanded the room with her deep, husky – and quite terrifying – voice. The scripts got passed round, butterflies in my stomach were building as the nerves and adrenaline took hold. I could not wait for her to bellow my name and call the part I was reading for; eventually she did.

When I got to the end of the first scene, I looked up.

I remember seeing the faces of the other people, some of whom were women that must have been about my mother's age, staring back at me. Some looked awkward, others sympathetic. 'Let's try that again, shall we, Polly?' Dorothea barked. What had gone wrong? I tried again, and the second time I looked up and felt relief. Those awkward, sympathetic looks had been replaced with smiles. 'Better,' Dorothea remarked. I thought I had tried my best, but once again I did not get the lead role. As usual, I was assigned the part of a villager.

However, I never gave up trying and a couple of years later I did get my moment. I had to stand in for the lead role in rehearsals and not only did I know every move, I knew every word; I had memorised the whole script even though my part only had about five lines. Finally, I gained a smile and some recognition from Dorothea, and after that I was lucky enough to get the lead role in other plays.

But that audition night has stayed with me. Only now do I feel I am starting to unravel and understand why those people at the audition were staring at me with such awkwardness and sympathy: I was eleven years old, but still could not read properly.***

I remember the huge sense of joy and accomplishment as I sat in my childhood bedroom and turned the last page of *The Empire of the Sun* – not a novel of note, or much of an achievement to many, but it was the first book I had ever managed to read from beginning to end on my own. It had taken an age, but I would often flick through after I had finished, admiring its vast number of pages.

I think about how I was always cut short by the teacher when reading aloud in English lessons. In exams, I would get my head down and write and write, only to feel it all unravel and the panic set in as I reread the question at the end and realised that I had misinterpreted it and not answered it correctly at all. I would leave the exams avoiding any "how did it go" conversations with friends.

School just wasn't for me. As soon as I arrived at secondary school, I felt ready to leave. I had great friendships, but no respect for the teachers; I felt they had written me off. Maybe this was because I showed none of the academic prowess that my sister did. The school was extremely proud and vocal about her going on to Cambridge University. And as supportive as my parents were, and I never felt compared to my sister, I do remember my mum always saying in her softly spoken voice, 'Well, you'll just have to try harder next time.'

By the age of 14, I felt I had outgrown school. The longing for some independence led to the decision to leave school at 16 and go to college for my A levels. A fresh start with no expectations gave me the power to start forging my own path: I could drive myself there, wear what I wanted, sit outside in the sunshine and smoke during lessons if I wanted to – no one cared whether I turned up or not.

A level results day came, along with a feeling I was getting used to – academic disappointment. This time my parents didn't hide their sadness either. My first response was to say, 'I don't care, I'll just become an air hostess,' like my mum had been. However, no longer did stewardessing offer the glamorous life she had always described, so my mum, more undeterred than I, got straight on to the phone and found a university place for me through clearing.

Seeing another opportunity for more independence and a chance to move away from home, off I went for another three years of education to study Corporate Communications. Enjoying it more than I had expected, I lived the usual student life of fitting in some work around a very busy social life! Unsurprisingly, I still didn't show the signs of being a high-achieving academic, but I scraped through and came out with a 2:1. Finally a result I could be proud of.

With the promise of never putting myself in the situation where I would have to sit an exam again, I started the job hunt!

A few months later, on a sunny June afternoon, I was sitting on the edge of my single mattress balanced on pallets, in Primrose Hill, ready to start my internship in a design agency. I didn't care that my room was tiny, or that I had the wardrobe space fit for a small child. I finally felt the independence that I'd craved for years. I had arrived, and I was ready for the real world.

And what an eye-opener it all was. Like many London design agencies at that time, they knew how to work hard and party harder. I said 'yes' to every project and worked on leading brand and retail campaigns that every household would recognise. I also said 'yes' to every night out, every party, every private member's club invite. I loved it all.

Amazingly, all the late nights didn't seem to distract from my dedication, enthusiasm and determination to do a great job. Even as a junior, the first shoots of my previously unseen ambitious side started to show.

I didn't have a plan then, and still don't, twenty-five years later. I've never been able to answer the question: 'What does the next five years of your career look like?' Yet in all my roles, however junior or senior, I have always been desperate to deliver the best for the agency and clients, whether this meant long hours, ripping it up and starting again, challenging colleagues, or telling people it was not good enough. Even when it got to the stage of owning my agency, it wasn't a power thing; it was a genuine desire to be the best we could. Perhaps I'm haunted by the idea of always needing to do better.

Just six years ago, I was stopped in my tracks. My boss pulled me to the side and told me, 'Soften your edges; you're too hard for our business, the team can't handle it.' I was stunned; he had employed me to make money and generate business, and that is exactly what I had been doing. Surely *I* wasn't the problem; it was the others that were too soft. In full view of the office, I walked out of the meeting room, trying to hold it together.

As hard as it was to hear, I was becoming too senior to ignore it. I realised that some self-reflection was needed, something that I had never found easy. I had to begin to recognise that maybe my way wasn't the only way, so I acted on the feedback.

A week later, nervously waiting at a table in a small private member's bar, it felt more like I was on a blind date instead of at a counselling session. Amazingly, Susie didn't make it feel like either. We clicked. I could be honest and open. She listened, delved deeper, asked uncomfortable questions and often challenged my thinking. If I thought the truth hurt from my boss, the level of honesty and transparency Susie went to was a lot more personal and hard-hitting. It meant that there were many times when I left via the loo to stop crying and try to gather myself together again. Other times I left feeling pumped and ready to take on the world. As time went on, thankfully the latter became more common.

Very early on in our sessions, Susie was able to figure me out better than I ever had myself. One thing she quickly taught me was that I had been blinded by my attitude. I was putting the same pressures on others as I did on myself, always striving for perfection. An unrealistic way to gain the best from people and often made for an uncomfortable environment too. I was not very empathetic in how I would share my opinions and feedback.

Perhaps, 'Well, you'll just have to try harder next time ...' was always playing somewhere in my head, and now I had taken it too far.

I focused on changing my behaviour, both to myself and to others, particularly in my pursuit of perfection, and people started to notice.

Colleagues could see a positive difference; one person actually asked whether I was in therapy.

But this process is still very much a work in progress, and it always will be. Even now, I am conscious on a daily basis not to slip backwards. Hopefully age is helping me mellow slightly too. I haven't been told to "soften my edges" since, but I do occasionally sit at my desk and shudder about how I used to be.

Over the years I've been asked by a number of colleagues if I'm dyslexic; I am pretty certain I am. It wasn't ever recognised while I was at school as it is now. Over time, I have learned techniques to address my challenges, like changing sentence structures to reduce the stress of using the right grammar or punctuation. I also make more phone calls than the average person to avoid having to write another email, and I will never ever read aloud in any situation. Even now, I will wake up at night thinking we've invested thousands of pounds at work to answer a client's problem and I have misinterpreted the brief, by not reading and understanding what it actually says.

In my thirties I had already started to enjoy financial gains in my career and was finding my feet in another Soho agency. One day, the business went through an unexpected change, which led to all the directors walking out. The outcome for me was a sudden promotion and a sizeable pay rise (the directors probably envisaged the mammoth task ahead better than I had). The initial pride and excitement quickly disappeared, and the reality of trying to run a pretty broken company, service many unhappy clients, and sell a story to employees of exciting times full of opportunity quickly began to take its toll.

The strain of constantly pitching for work, mixed with resignation letters and recruiting for "new blood", started to show through long hours, pitted with quick, discreet visits to the pub with a couple of the other new directors who were also feeling the pressure. The late nights working would often be followed by leaving Soho bars in the early hours of the morning.

Feeling trapped, and exhausted, in the hamster wheel, friends started to say they didn't recognise me; I seemed continuously stressed and distracted. I didn't like what I could see either, but walking away, feeling as if I had failed, didn't seem an option.

However, the wake-up call no one ever wants came while I was at a client's wedding. My oldest, closest friend called to tell me her amazing mum, someone who was such a big part of my childhood, had suddenly passed away. I rushed immediately to be with her and her dad, and was shocked by the first thing her dad said to me: 'We're all so worried about you, Polly, you're working too hard, it's not good for you.'

The sadness and his words consumed me for days; saying goodbye to someone I loved and adored and seeing the heartbreak of those left behind was so difficult. So, with a new perspective, I resigned.

I was feeling free and fearless and surprised that I had no sense of failure, just relief.

The unexpected career break did not concern me, in fact I was looking forward to a few months off with no plans. However, it was short-lived, as an old colleague asked me to become their business partner in a small marketing agency (ironically called Ambition). As someone who isn't an overthinker, within weeks I had remortgaged, invested and was now a co-owner of an agency. The following six years were intense, growing the agency to be award-winning and gaining some prestigious brand names as clients; the company had expanded well, and we were reaping the rewards.

However, it had become my identity; I was too emotionally invested and committed to work. I was using it as a crutch for the things I was missing, and it was really starting to show. With another failed personal relationship under my belt, this was the catalyst for some more self-reflection.

You would think that being a business owner would allow for life decisions to be easier, but more long hours, weekend work and the continual stress of a balance sheet wasn't the greatest environment. Added to this were the flaws in the relationship with my business partner, with lack of communication, collaboration, and trust playing too strong a part to ignore. But walking away from something commercially successful did not seem right either. Once again, I wasn't feeling happy or satisfied. It had become all-consuming, and not in a healthy way.

After nine months working behind the scenes with a mentor and lawyer, it was time for me to make my exit, again, with no job to go to. Now I was ready to have some real time out and reconsider what my future could look like. I could see my resilience was growing, and I knew I didn't have to jump into making my next career decision.

Time out, with no plan. I thought, fleetingly, that I should move to New York City. and become an interior designer. Instead, I decided to stop, and listen to the loudest thing in my head: the ticking of my body clock. Something I couldn't continue to ignore.

I was now 38 and it had become apparent that the tears and self-pity I had felt in recent years were the grieving for not being in the right situation to be able to start a family, like so many of my close friends were. Also, I had just been thrown another curve ball. When I was 14, I underwent major surgery to have my back straightened. At 16, I had to have the operation again, as I'd broken the metal rods. For the following twenty years, my back had been doing fine and I had got used to any daily aches and pains. But one day, in the office, I turned to walk into a busy meeting room and instantly knew, when the immediate burning, sickness and then fear flooded through my body, that something in my back had just moved. Shaken and knowing this was not good news, I nevertheless continued as normal, ignoring the problem. However, the sensations in my back became more and more frequent, and a best friend – who saw me flinching with every movement of my spine – eventually persuaded me to see a consultant.

Apparently, I was really lucky I could still stand and walk. I should never have taken up running, let alone completed a marathon. He estimated that in ten years I would not be able to walk or stand properly and I would need the front of my spine rebuilt, not a small procedure. Through my tears I mumbled, 'But I want a baby.' He told me that my back wouldn't be strong enough to hold a pregnancy for a minimum of two years post-operation, and suggested that I 'get my head out of the sand, walk out of here, and get pregnant ASAP.' For weeks I cried, feeling more self-pity, and it seemed that the forgotten fear and pain of twenty years ago was very much buried inside of me.

With time not on my side, my decision was made. I was going to try for a baby. On my own.

I shocked myself by the confidence and defiance with which I told people this was my plan. Years ago, I would have been embarrassed for fear of judgement or being talked about, with people saying there was something wrong with me for not having found my lifelong partner. But now, heading into my forties, I was proud and excited for what the future could hold. Many friends and colleagues were behind me, offering support and encouragement in so many ways. I certainly wasn't listening to any comments and whispers saying, 'It's not God's creation' or, 'What will other people think?' These were not things that kept me up at night. While I knew there was a risk that having a sperm donor child might fracture my immediate family bond, I was undeterred by some of the narrow-minded comments I had heard; my drive and determination became stronger.

At this time, embarking on single motherhood, I decided it was not the right moment to change my career path or move countries, and so I started work in another London agency. I did not miss being the company owner, my drive was still as strong as if it was my own. I did wonder for a brief time why I still wanted another leadership role, putting myself in a new situation in which I had to earn respect and show my worth.

I was undeterred by being the only senior woman in the company, and quickly realised I could add value to the team. In my whole career, I have been fortunate never to feel like I've been fighting in a man's world. Instead, I have been respected for what I bring as a person and as a female to the business. (This is not always the same outside of work, where men have expressed to me their surprise that senior females are often taken so seriously at work – an opinion that enrages me and I hope fades fast so future generations do not have to battle with such outdated stereotypes.)

I was definitely pushing myself out of my comfort zones and standing up when I didn't think something or someone was being dealt with in the right way. This is something that Susie has constantly helped me to do, and she has continued to advise me on the best way to approach things and encouraged me to have more self-belief. I am sure this was also due to the fact that I was now a very happy and grateful mother of an incredible little girl. I sailed through a back-pain-free pregnancy, with no need for a day off work until a week before her due date. The feeling of utter joy and contentment that washed over me when she arrived was magical. The moment I had dreamed of was now a reality, and through all the career moves and 'climbing the ladder', this was by far my proudest and greatest achievement.

Motherhood and work seemed to blend well together; I felt I was making a success of both. With the support of an incredible au pair, I seemed to be able to retain my independence and didn't feel as if I had lost my sense of self, which I know is not the case for a lot of new mums.

The first two years of my daughter's life sped past. During that time my company went through many different iterations, with various senior hires, not all of them positive ones. Through this, I was more and more at the helm of the business, making lots of difficult and challenging decisions for the company; this was being recognised and I was asked to become the managing director.

I turned it down. It just didn't feel the right time for me to say yes. The money and status weren't the driving reasons behind my decisions anymore. I realised that what I really wanted was time with my daughter, so I resigned. Luckily, in hindsight, my resignation was not accepted. Instead, we agreed to a five-month sabbatical.

Travelling with my daughter on safari, riding on elephant back, swimming in turquoise seas and taking in the sights and sounds of many different countries was the most adventurous and relaxing thing I had done in years. We could not have been luckier with our timings, we returned to the UK, and me to work, two weeks before the COVID-19 pandemic hit the world!

With a clear head and renewed vigour, I came back to show that I was still 100% committed. The break could not have been better timed. And now firing on all cylinders again, I am the Managing Director and feel this is the right time for me to succeed.

Who knows what the future holds from here, but I am grateful I didn't follow my parents' friends' predictions of an early pregnancy. Becoming a mother at 41 has taught me so much. I am now far more appreciative of what I have and of the people around me. I am still determined and driven, but each day I am slowly starting to realise that I'm doing OK. I do wonder, as I am just about to start a house renovation, whether I will ever be someone who will go in the slow lane, but for now it feels right to keep my foot down. Maybe it's time now too to focus on myself and look for Mr Right and, more importantly, someone who can be the best father figure to an already very independent four-year-old!

It is nine years now since leaving the consultant's office and my back is showing no obvious signs of giving up anytime soon – the same way I feel about my career.

Postscript

AND A RESPONSE TO POLLY FROM SUSIE

> I am still determined and driven, but each day I am slowly
> starting to realise that I'm doing OK.

Polly

Supporting other people's careers has been my 'career' for the past two decades, and it's been wonderful. I don't like the noun 'career'. The dictionary tells us it's about progress in two ways: a journey through time and an opportunity to develop. I like that definition but, like all definitions, it's pretty limiting. Limiting because all these stories reveal so much more.

Polly's story is last in this book and there is a reason for this. I feel it's a brilliantly honest account of a life well lived. A life that is (everything crossed) only halfway through. A journey that is brave, experimental and often doesn't go according to plan. Just like mine and maybe yours too? It illustrates how work and life are inextricably linked. The story holds lessons for us all and highlights important themes to reflect on in working life today.

Polly's early life impacted her career identity. She arrived for her first day in the office with a whole set of beliefs, possibly misconceptions, about who she was and what she might offer the world. Polly had struggled with conventional academic markers of success but was a striver, always receiving an 'A' for effort. The hard worker, but never quite marked for high office. How wrong that was.

You bring your whole self to work and this self, like Polly, has been moulded by early life experience. When I worked at the London School of Economics, we had a term for our graduating students: 'oven-ready' candidates. I always felt this was problematic. On the outside you come clutching your hard-won qualifications and wearing your Sunday best, but underneath this glossy exterior you are a laundry bag of life scripts, dramas, celebrations and tragedy.

Borrowing the language of therapy, we are a glorious mixture of a 'trauma' self, a 'survival' self and a 'healthy' self. Recognising and accepting these identities is part of our life journey. When Polly feels good and 'healthy' at work she feels grounded and at ease. She thinks clearly and expresses herself fluently. She empathises and listens well, processing her own emotional reaction, but not letting it overwhelm her. Polly's 'trauma' self is more split off, when her emotions are frozen and her 'survival' self's job is to maintain that split boundary. When Polly acknowledges her burnout at work, she knows that her survival self has taken over. But she is brave and decisive enough to realise that she has to step away and regroup. As she arrives for coaching, she recognises that she has moved into a judgmental and less compassionate way of being and she commits to experimenting with a healthier way of relationship building. I use this example because it's an illustration of Polly's commitment to deepen her self-understanding. It's the cornerstone of thriving at work. She is thinking deeply about how she understands, engages and interacts with those around her. She is on a journey to being her 'best' self and using her unique style to best effect. I salute her striving to genuinely grow both as a leader and as a person. Indeed all the writers in the book possess this desire to reach their potential, whatever this might be.

Polly doesn't have a life plan. Her career has unfolded chapter by chapter. I did have a client who had an excel spreadsheet for her life. This year to get married, this year for promotion, this year for having a child ... and so on. We sense this approach might end in tears. Never has there been a time when experimentation was more of a necessity. You can be a conscious career driver when you have developed greater levels of self-awareness and now have a sense of who you are and what you want. However, this isn't static, we all have multiple identities and there won't only be that one perfect role or opportunity out there for you. Polly has asked the powerful question: 'Out of the many possible selves I might become what attracts me most now?' She was brave enough to walk away from her own business, understanding that it wasn't serving her anymore.

You will have read stories in the book about what happens when work and career isn't a smooth ride and some of the writers have revealed their own vulnerability. You are a 'work in progress' and this should help you to be compassionate with yourself and understand that it's OK when you are falling short. It's an essential part of the human condition. As Polly shares, 'I was too emotionally invested and committed to work. I was using it as a crutch for the things I was missing, and it was really starting to show'. When you are feeling vulnerable it allows you to step back and to ask the big questions that are vital for your career development; questions such as, 'What do I want?' 'What do I care about?' 'How do I want to behave at work?' 'What does it mean to take advantage of my greatest strengths?'

Sometimes you will recognise when your life is out of balance and something is missing. Polly wanted to have a child and undertook this mammoth venture as a single parent. Becoming a parent changes many things, but it also sets the context for a novel approach to working life. Polly brings her learning from motherhood into her work: 'I am now far more appreciative of what I have and of the people around me. I am still determined and driven, but each day I am slowly starting to realise that I'm doing OK.' This learning doesn't, of course, only come from parenthood; I have emerged from a decade of dedicated hard work determined to shift the balance of my life. Reflecting on what my deepest values are means I can be kinder to myself and spend three hours digging a vegetable bed in the community garden or crawling around on my knees with my young grandson.

All of the storytellers in this book haven't necessarily made this explicit, but they have turned their dreams into reality by applying tremendous consistency. It might make me sound rather old fashioned, but I'm not sure there is much substitute for this one. At the beginning of your career you are often lacking a strategy as you just absorb and learn. It's a bit later on that you join the dots and become more consciously strategic about what you want your work to look like. As Polly realised, none of us want work to be our only focus. However there are times when you do need to get your head down and focus on getting better and better or on building assets that you can deploy in the future. As you focus on your 'craft' and thinking about how you can become more skilled, your thinking will shift from, 'What can the world offer me? to 'What can I offer the world?'

I hope that the stories in the book have inspired you to reflect on your working life.

What will be your story?

Acknowledgements

I would like to thank all the writers who gave up so much of their time to write, rewrite, agonise and generally dig deep to get their story on paper. Thank you for supporting each other and encouraging me to keep on going!

Thank you to Lauretta Barrow and Cathal Cleary who have been provocative and insightful editors. Thank you to Karen Cogan who ran a brilliant writing workshop for the writers at the beginning of the project. Thank you to Sarah Bell who has challenged me to think about promoting the book and my work, specifically acting as a catalyst for the accompanying podcasts. Thank you to those writers who were entertaining and articulate podcast guests. And thank you to Daisy Grant for her patient and professional podcast production.

Thank you to all my clients who I have been lucky enough to work with. Each one of you has taught me something and has helped me to learn and develop my perspectives on working life.

Hugs and love to William, Sophie, Millie and Eliza. Love conquers all. Your encouragement, intellectual and emotional companionship kept the project alive.

Appendix A

SCHEIN'S CAREER ANCHORS

Edgar Henry Schein was a Swiss-born American business theorist and psychologist who was professor at the MIT Sloan School of Management.

Edgar Schein's Careers Anchors tool will build on your thinking about your values by looking in more detail at what is important to you in your career.

Use these links to find out more:
https://www.businessballs.com/self-management/career-anchors-edgar-schein/https://www.careeranchorsonline.com/SCA/about.do?open=prod https://rapidbi.com/careeranchors/

Here are the anchors:

Technical/Functional Competence
This kind of person likes being good at something and will work to become a guru or expert. They like to be challenged and then use their skill to meet the challenge, doing the job properly and better than almost anyone else.

General Managerial Competence
Unlike technical/functional people, these individuals want to be managers (and not just to get more money, although this may be used as a metric of success). They like problem-solving and dealing with other people. They thrive on responsibility. To be successful, they also need emotional competence.

Autonomy/Independence
These people have a primary need to work under their own rules and steam.

Security/Stability
Security-focused people seek stability and continuity as a primary factor of their lives. They avoid risks and are generally 'lifers' in their job.

Entrepreneurial Creativity
These individuals like to invent things, be creative and, most of all, to run their own businesses. They differ from those who seek autonomy in that they will share the workload. They find ownership very important. They easily get bored.

Service/Dedication to a Cause
Service-oriented people are driven by how they can help other people more than using their talents (which may fall in other areas). They are often drawn to an organisation with a strong quality of mission.

Pure Challenge
People driven by challenge seek constant stimulation and difficult problems that they can tackle. Such people will change jobs when the current one gets boring and their career can be very varied.

Lifestyle
Those who are focused first on lifestyle look at their whole pattern of living. They focus on balance and see work and life as integrally complementary. They may even take long periods off work in which to indulge in passions.

Appendix B

LIFELINE EXERCISE

How do I tell my career story?

Map out your career story to date.

Draw a curvy line across the page which details your career from leaving school until today. This curvy line will have highs and lows.

Take some time to think about what was happening for you in these periods.

- When were your most fulfilled moments?
- What are the common themes that link your happiest moments?
- What does your story tell you about what you are passionate about?
- When did you feel you were at your very best; that things were going well and somehow you didn't have to try too hard because you were being true to yourself?
- Conversely, what made you feel so angry / frustrated / fed up that you felt compelled to act?
- What were you prepared to stand up for? To be brave about? To stand firm on?

Notes

Chapter Two

i.   Whyte, David. Consolations: *The Solace, Nourishment and Underlying Meaning of Everyday Words*. Many Rivers Press, 2015.

ii.   Jeffers, Susan. Feel *The Fear And Do It Anyway*. Vermillion Life Essentials, 2012.

iii.   Ibarra, Hermina. *Working Identity: Unconventional Strategies For Reinventing Your Career*. Havard Business Review Press, 2004.

iv.   Brown, Brené. *Daring Greatly; How the Courage to Be Vulnerable Transforms the Way We Live, Love, Parent and Lead*. Avery, 2012.

v.   Orenstein GA, Lewis L. *Erikson's Stages of Psychosocial Development*. StatPearls Publishing, 2020. Available from: https://www.ncbi.nlm.nih.gov/books/NBK556096/

vi.   Bandura, Arthur. *Reflections on self-efficacy. In S. Rachman (Ed.) Advances in behaviour research and therapy* (Vol 1 pp. 237-269). Oxford: Pergamon Press, 1978.

vii.   Dufourmantelle, Anne. *Power of Gentleness: Meditations on the Risk of Living*. Fordham University Press, 2018.

Chapter Four

i.   Aristotle. *Introduction to Eudaimonia*. https://www.thecollector.com/aristotle-philosophy-virtue-ethics-eudaimonia/

ii.   Maslow, Abraham. *A Theory of Human Motivation*. Wilder Publications, 2022 and https://www.simplypsychology.org/maslow.html

iii.   Pink, Daniel. Drive: *The Surprising Truth About What Motivates Us*. Riverhead Hardcover, 2009.

iv.   Csikszentmihalyi, Mihaly. *Creativity: Flow and the Psychology of Discovery and Invention*. Harber Perennial, 2013.

v.   Seligman, Martin. Character Strengths survey https://www.viacharacter.org/

Chapter Six

i.   Beecher,Henry Ward. *Life Thoughts, Gathered From the Extemporaneous Discourses of Henry Ward Beecher by One of His Congregation*. University of Michigan Library, 2006.

ii. Radcliffe, Steve. *Leadership Plain and Simple*. 2nd ed. FT Publishing International, 2012.

Chapter Eight

i.   Carlyle,Thomas. *The Hero as a Man of Letters*. Kessinger Publishing, 2010.

ii. Aviva. Work life balance study:
     https://www.aviva.com/newsroom/news-releases/2022/08/work-life-balance-overtakes-salary-post-pandemic/

Chapter Ten

i.   Denborough, David and Ncube, Ncazelo. The Tree of Life concept.
     https://nathanbweller.com/tree-life-simple-exercise-reclaiming-identity-direction-life-story/

ii. Kegan, Robert. *The Evolving Self; Problem and Process in Human Development*. Harvard University Press, 1982.

iii. Frankl, Victor. *Man's Search for Meaning*. Beacon Press, 2000.

Chapter Twelve

i.   LV. 9m adults change jobs during Covid pandemic.
     https://www.lv.com/about-us/press/9m-adults-change-jobs-during-covid-pandemic

Chapter Fourteen

i.   Washington Post
     https://www.washingtonpost.com/lifestyle/magazine/the-midlife-doldrums-are-a-social-crisis-now-theres-momentum-for-some-radical-fixes/2018/04/10/c5674db8-2e96-11e8-8688-e053ba58f1e4_story.html

ii. Super, Donald E. A. *Theory of Vocational Development*. American Psychologist 8:185-190.1953.

iii. Orenstein GA, Lewis L. *Erikson's Stages of Psychosocial Development*. StatPearls Publishing, 2020. Available from: https://www.ncbi.nlm.nih.gov/books/NBK556096/

iv. Baltes, Paul, Lindenberger Ulman, Staudinger, Ursula. Volume I. Theoretical Models of Human Development https://doi.org/10.1002/9780470147658.chpsy0111 2007.

v. Kegan, Robert. *The Evolving Self; Problem and Process in Human Development*. Harvard University Press, 1982.

Chapter Seventeen

i. https://eu.themyersbriggs.com/en/tools/MBTI?gclid=CjwKCAjwr_uCBhAFEiwAX8YJgQZkU9cBWeQrYCuszhq4-Dvwx-9rj5I9EIKKjpl0kH78Cjvsj_ws9RoCDWwQAvD_BwE

ii. Reed Turrell, Emma. *Please Yourself: How to Stop People-Pleasing and Transform the Way You Live* (p.2). HarperCollins Publishers. Kindle Edition

iiii. David, Susan. Recognizing Your Emotions as Data, Not Directives. LinkedIn, 21 February 2021https://www.linkedin.com/pulse/recognizing-your-emotions-data-directives-susan-david-ph-d-/?trk=public_profile_article_view

iv. Dweck, Carol. Mindset: *The New Psychology of Success*. New York, Ballantine Books, 2008.

v. Perel, Ester. How's Work. https://howswork.estherperel.com/episodes/prologue

Chapter Twenty-two

i. Lamott, Anne. *Bird by Bird*: *Instructions on Writing and Life*. Knopf Doubleday Publishing Group, 1995.

ii. Hewitt, Paul., Flett, Gordon. Perfectionism: *A Relational Approach to Conceptualization, Assessment, and Treatment*. Guilford Press, 2017.

iii. Gilbert, Elizabeth. *Big Magic: Creative Living beyond Fear*. Bloomsbury Paperbacks, 2016.

iv.   McCrea, Sean., Liberman, Nira.,Trope, Yaacov., Sherman, Steven. Construal Level and Procrastination. University of Konstanz, Tel Aviv University, New York University, and Indiana University Journal of Psychological Science, 2008.

Milton Keynes UK
Ingram Content Group UK Ltd.
UKHW020618041123
431893UK00018B/724

9 781789 633764